A Call to Delaying Sinners
by Thomas Doolittle
with chapters by C. Matthew McMahon

Copyright Information

A Call to Delaying Sinners, by Thomas Doolittle, with chapters by C. Matthew McMahon
Edited by Therese B. McMahon

Copyright ©2020 by Puritan Publications and A Puritan's Mind™

Some language and grammar have been updated from the original manuscript. Any change in wording or punctuation has not changed the intent or meaning of the original authors, and has been made to aid the modern reader.

Published by Puritan Publications
A Ministry of A Puritan's Mind™ in Crossville, TN.
www.apuritansmind.com
www.puritanpublications.com

All rights reserved. No part of this publication may be reproduced, stored in a retrieval system or transmitted in any form by any means, electronic, mechanical, photocopy, recording or otherwise, without the prior permission of the publisher, except as provided by USA copyright law.

This Print Edition, 2020
Electronic Edition, 2020
Manufactured in the United States of America

ISBN: 978-1-62663-361-2
eISBN: 978-1-62663-360-5

Table of Contents

An Exhortation on this Work 4

Meet Thomas Doolittle 6

To the Reader 13

Sermon 1 Coming to Christ in Haste 23

Sermon 2 Now or Never 34

Sermon 3 Repent Today 45

Sermon 4 Stop Your Sinning 58

Sermon 5 Young and Old 68

Sermon 6 Slow in Coming 83

Sermon 7 Isn't God Merciful? 98

Sermon 8 Take God for Your God 114

Appendix: A Covenant Made with God 122

Other Helpful Books by Puritan Publications 126

An Exhortation on this Work
by C. Matthew McMahon, Ph.D., Th.D.

Sometimes, republished puritan works need no introduction. Once you read this work, you will agree that Doolittle's work doesn't need any help or introduction at all; just a little exhortation to soak him in. It *may be* that you are unfamiliar with Doolittle himself. The bio in the next chapter will alleviate that. He is a favorite as it relates to puritan sermons that dig deep into your soul. His *Captives Bound in Chains Made Free by Christ* on Isaiah 61:1 is monumental to the freedom that sinners can have in Jesus Christ. His *Love to Christ Necessary to Escape the Curse at His Coming* is soul inspiring and should be read by every believer. His work, *The Saint's Convoy to, and Mansions in Heaven* is a manual of divine comfort. Yes, in reading Doolittle, one comes away with all the necessary elements of hearing a concerned minister of the Gospel, one among a thousand, who can show a man his righteousness and sin, and can preach Christ freely and with great power. 400 years later, the Spirit of God is still attending the words he preached which house the marrow of Scripture in the preaching of this godly man, and the Lord is still working through his sermons and into the souls of readers and hearers. Truly, he needs no introduction; *just letting him loose on your soul will be enough.*

    This particular work of Doolittle is a gem. It was originally a series of sermons preached to his congregation, which he then took and combined into a uniform book (this is the book you are now reading). In laying this book out, I have taken and separated these sermons into their respective chapters. There are 8 sermons, each building upon the former, and all surrounding the need to hasten and come to Jesus Christ quickly. They are short, but commanding and authoritative. His central text is taken from Psalm 119:60, "I made haste, and delayed not to keep thy commandments." The sermons cover his main doctrine, which stands as this: *that what the blessed and eternal God commands us to do, is to be done with all possible speed, with all haste, without delay.* Doolittle utilizes his time to deal practically with calling unconverted sinners to come to Christ, and exhorting converted sinners to make the most of their time since they have been graciously saved.

Doolittle was a faithful servant of Christ whose preaching and writing were used to awaken many sinners to the religious business of eternal life and eternal death. This is evident on every page of the book and is a full testimony to the exactness of his biblical preaching.

In the Grace of Christ's Saving Mercy,
C. Matthew McMahon, Ph.D., Th.D.
From my study, June, 2020

Meet Thomas Doolittle
Edited by C. Matthew McMahon

Thomas Doolittle (1632–1707) was a nonconformist tutor and preacher, third son of Anthony Doolittle (a glover), was born at Kidderminster in 1632 or the latter half of 1631. While at the grammar school of his native town, he heard Richard Baxter preach as lecturer (appointed April 5, 1641) the sermons afterwards published as "The Saint's Everlasting Rest" (1653). These sermons were used by God to produce his conversion. Placed with a country attorney, he scrupled at copying writings on Sunday, and went home determined not to become a lawyer. Baxter encouraged him to enter the ministry. He was admitted as an undergraduate at Pembroke Hall, Cambridge, on June 7, 1649, being then "17 *annos natus.*"[1] His tutor was William Moses, afterwards ejected from the mastership of Pembroke. Doolittle graduated with an M.A. at Cambridge. Leaving the university for London, he became popular as a preacher, and in preference to other candidates was chosen (in 1653) as their pastor by the parishioners of St. Alphage, London Wall.[2] Doolittle received Presbyterian ordination. During the nine years of his tenure he fully sustained his popularity. On the passing of the Act of Uniformity (1662) he "upon the whole thought it his duty to be a nonconformist." He was poor; the day after his farewell sermon a parishioner gave him a welcome present of 20£. A residence had been built for Doolittle, but it appears to have been private property; it neither went to his successor, Matthew Fowler, D.D., nor did Doolittle continue to enjoy it. He moved to Moorfields and opened a boarding-school, which succeeded so well that he took a larger house in Bunhill Fields, where he was assisted by Thomas Vincent, who was ejected from St. Mary Magdalene Church, Milk Street.

---

[1] He could not, therefore, have been born in 1630, as stated in his "memoirs." The source of the error is that another Thomas, son of William and Jane Doolittle, was baptized at Kidderminster on October 20, 1630.

[2] The living is described as sequestered in Rastrick's list as quoted by Palmer, but James Halsey, D.D., the deprived rector, had been dead twelve or thirteen years.

Sermon 1: Coming to Christ in Haste

In the year of the plague (1665) Doolittle and his pupils removed to Woodford Bridge, near Chigwell, close to Epping Forest, Vincent remaining behind. Returning to London in 1666, Doolittle was one of the nonconformist ministers who, in defiance of the law, erected preaching-places when churches were lying in ruins after the great fire. His first meeting-house (probably a wooden structure) was in Bunhill Fields, and here he was undisturbed. But when he transferred his congregation to a large and substantial building (the first of the kind in London, if not in England) which he had erected in Mugwell (now Monkwell) Street, the authorities set the law in motion against him. The lord mayor amicably endeavored to persuade him to desist from preaching; he declined. On the following Saturday about midnight his door was broken open by a force sent to arrest him. He escaped over a wall, and intended to preach next day. From this he was dissuaded by his friends, one of whom (Thomas Sare, ejected from Rudford, Gloucestershire) took his place in the pulpit. The sermon was interrupted by the appearance of a body of troops. As the preacher stood his ground "the officer bid his men to fire." "Shoot, if you please," was the reply. There was a considerable uproar, but no arrests were made. The meeting-house, however, was taken possession of in the name of the king, and for some time was utilized as a lord mayor's chapel. On the indulgence of March 15, 1672 Doolittle took out a license for his meeting-house. The original document, dated April 2nd, hangs in Dr. Williams's library. The meeting-house is described as "a certain room adjoining to the dwelling-house of Thomas Doolittle in Mugwell Street." Doolittle owned the premises, but he now resided in Islington, where his school had developed into an academy for "university learning." When Charles II (March 8, 1673) broke the seal of his declaration of indulgence, thus invalidating the licenses granted under it, Doolittle conducted his academy with great caution at Wimbledon. His biographers represent this removal as a consequence of the passing (it may have been an instance of the enforcing) of the *Five Miles Act* (in 1665). At Wimbledon he had a narrow escape from arrest. He returned to Islington before 1680, but in 1683 he was again dislodged. He removed to Battersea (where his goods were seized), and then to Clapham. These migrations destroyed his academy, but not before he had contributed to the education of some men of notation. Matthew Henry, Samuel Bury, Thomas Emlyn, and Edmund Calamy, D.D., were among his pupils. Two of his students, John Kerr, M.D., and Thomas Rowe, achieved distinction as nonconformist tutors. The academy was at an end in 1687, when Doolittle lived at St. John's Court, Clerkenwell, and had Calamy a second time under his care for some months as a boarder. Until the death of his wife he still continued to receive students for the ministry, but apparently not more than one at a time. His last pupil was Nathaniel Humphreys.

The Toleration Act of 1689 left Doolittle free to resume his services at Mugwell Street, preaching twice every Sunday and lecturing on Wednesdays. Vincent, his assistant, had died in 1678; later he had as assistants his pupil, John Mottershead (removed to Ratcliff Cross), his son, Samuel Doolittle (removed to Reading), and Daniel Wilcox, who succeeded him.

Doolittle's private covenant of personal religion (Nov. 18, 1693) occupies six closely printed folio pages. He had long suffered from gallstones and other infirmities, but his last illness was very brief. He preached and catechized with great vigor on Sunday, May 18th, took to his bed in the latter part of the week, lay for two days unconscious, and died on May 24th, 1707. He was the last survivor of the London ejected clergy.

Six portraits of Doolittle have been engraved; one represents him in his own hair "ætatis suæ 52;" another, older and in a bushy wig, has less expression. The latter was engraved by James Caldwall for the first edition of

Palmer (1775), from a painting in the possession of S. Sheaf or Sheafe, Doolittle's grandson; in the second edition a worthless substitute is given.

Doolittle married in 1653, shortly after his ordination; his wife died in 1692. Of his family of three sons and six daughters, all except a daughter, were dead in 1723.

Doolittle's twenty publications are carefully enumerated at the close of the "Memoirs" (1723), probably by Jeremiah Smith. They begin with (1) "Sermon on Assurance in the Morning Exercise at Cripplegate," 1661, 4to, and consist of sermons and devotional treatises, of which (2) "A Treatise concerning the Lord's Supper," 1665, 12mo (portrait by R. White), and (3) "A Call to Delaying Sinners," 1683, 12mo, went through many editions. His latest work published in his lifetime was (4) "The Saint's Convoy to, and Mansions in Heaven," 1698, 8vo. Posthumous was (5) "A Complete Body of Practical Divinity," *etc.* 1723, fol. (the editors say this volume was the product of his Wednesday catechetical lectures, "catechising was his special excellency and delight;" the list of subscribers includes several clergymen of the established church). One of his most vibrant sermon series, later turned into a tract, was "Captives Bound in Chains Made Free by Christ Their Surety", 1674. Also, his work "The Swearer Silenced" in 1674 was made popular.

For Further Study:

Funeral Sermon by Daniel Williams, D.D., 1707; Calamy's *Account*, 1713, pp. 52, 331; Continuation, 1727, pp. 75, 506; Hist. of my own Life, 2nd edit. 1830, i. 105, 138, ii. 78; Walker's *Sufferings*, 1714, pt. ii. p. 171; Tong's *Life of Matthew Henry*, 1716; *Memoirs* prefixed to *Body of Divinity*, 1723; *Memoir of T. Emlyn* prefixed to his *Works*, 4th edit. 1746, i. 7; *Protestant Dissenters'* Mag. 1799, p. 392; Palmer's *Nonconf. Memorial*, 2nd edit. 1802, i. 86; Toulmin's *Hist. View of Prot. Diss.* 1814, pp. 237, 584; Granger's *Biog. Hist. of England*, 1824, v. 67; Lee's *Diaries and Letters of P. Henry*, 1882, p. 334, *etc.*; Jeremy's *Presbyterian Fund*, 1885, pp. 7, 12, *etc.*; information from records of Presbyterian Board, by W.D. Jeremy; extract from Pembroke College Records per the Rev. C.E. Searle, D.D., and from parish register, Kidderminster, per Mr. R. Grove.

To the Reader

Christian Reader,

There is no Christian living, but is sufficiently satisfied, and does very well know that repentance and reconciliation to God is the one thing necessary. The indispensable duty of every man and woman that desires to be saved must have both. Yet such has been, and more especially in this present generation, is the miserable depravity of human nature, that we are far too apt to defer that until the very last, that ought to be our first and chief care and endeavor. To enforce and convince you of the necessity of this great duty, is the design of this treatise. There was never a greater need for it than now. When men are so far from making this their greatest care and concern, that they can hardly spare a thought on their eternal salvation. For enforcing this most necessary duty on the hearts and minds of Christians, the following sermons are very useful and expedient. The time and opportunity of receiving grace may easily slip away. It is therefore the duty of every Christian to lay hold on the present opportunity, and to receive the grace of Christ now, instantly, while grace is to be had. The learned Pharisees could not discern their opportunity by discerning the signs of his coming, and you have it in Matthew 19 at the beginning, neither could the Jews know their opportunity, for it was hidden from their eyes, as you may read in Luke 19:42. Opportunity is hardly embraced. Therefore, it becomes every wise man to lay hold of the times and not

Sermon 1: Coming to Christ in Haste

let it pass, unless he hereafter sorely repent on account of it.

But who is the man, Solomon asks? (Eccles. 8:1ff). That is, how rarely is the wiseman to be found? For the wise man, he says, discerns time and judgment. That is to say he is able to discern when things are to be done, and therefore it's rare to find such a wiseman in the voyage to heaven. *It is hard to save our tide.* Not one in a thousand lets it slip. The improving of this therefore is a man's greatest wisdom, (Deut. 32:29). O! that they were wise, that they understood this, that they would consider their latter end. The wise man's heart is said to be in his right hand. That is, the wisdom of his heart teaches him to manage his affairs judiciously, and in season. That man, who though he is never so wise and prudent in the world and worldly things, yet if he does not have wisdom to know the season of grace, he well may be described as a fool, and will so appear to be this into all eternity. And do you not think it will cause you the greatest torment and vexation imaginable to that man, who when he comes to die, shall be compelled to say, "O! I was never so wise, who was wise for everything, but to save my soul?"

Men must lay hold of the present opportunity in that which facilitates every action and employment, making a work come off smoothly and with facility. The gracious God, if we embrace an opportunity, offers to help us, and work with us. O! the goodness of a merciful God, that though he set us so light and easy a task, yet offers to work with us too! A burden is more light and easy, when two people assist in carrying it, then it would be on the back of a single person. When the boat has the advantage both of wind and tide, to carry it forward, it goes easily and pleasantly on. This is the case of that Christian, who seasonably embraces the offers of grace and mercy. He has the assistance of the Holy Spirit, for obtaining his desired happiness. To lay hold of the present opportunity, makes every action look beautiful. It makes all our performances look on with a lovely grace, (Eccl. 3:11), "He hath made every thing beautiful in its time." Know that fruit gathered in season is the pleasantest fruit, and that a word spoken in season of obtaining grace is *a word up and spinning on its wheels*. When the season of obtaining grace is past, our endeavors are unpleasant to God, as well as unprofitable to us. Nor is that all, but we are accountable for every action we commit, and for the time we do it. Eccl. 11:9, "Rejoice O young man in thy youth, and let thy heart cheer thee in the days of thy youth, and walk in the ways of thy heart, and in the sight of thine eyes," but now, though, for all these things, God will bring you to judgment. Where you see he shall be not only judged by his actions, but for the time he misspent. O! that every Christian would lay this seriously to heart, and contemplate in this way with himself. "O wretch that I am! How many holy sabbaths have I profaned! And how many oaths have I sworn! How many hundred times have I neglected prayer, to call on God! How many times have I derided godliness! How many lies have I told!" And if for every idle word you must give an account, certainly for every sermon, sabbath and ordinance, under which you have been idle, you shall not escape without a reckoning.

Moreover, neglecting of opportunity is the greatest destroyer in the world. It is not so much being bad, as the delaying to be good, that destroys most. It is not the flat denials, but foolish delays that ruin Christians, Eccl. 8:6, "Because to every purpose there is time and judgment," therefore, the misery of man is great on him. Few deny, but most delay to be saved.

We see opportunity is embraced by all people in their meanest concerns, and shall not a Christian much more lay hold on all opportunities for the salvation of his soul? Does not the farmer observe his seasons? Does not the merchant observe his? Does not the seaman observe the seas? Yes, the very workers of iniquity observe opportunities and seasons in which they may perform their delights, and shall the only precious opportunities for the good of our souls be neglected? This delaying in the pursuit of salvation is a delaying to be freed from the greatest evil, *viz.*, the wrath of God, guilt, damnation, and hell.

Therefore, O Christians, let it be your great and immediate care to man your peace between God and your own souls. Do not neglect the least time, but even today, while it is called today, lay hold of and embrace the offers of Christ in the Gospel.

There are thousands that have been servants of sin all their days, and though the pains and diseases of their old age convince them that the pleasures of sin are but for a season, yet they will remain constant and faithful to their master's service and die the devil's martyrs. They are so far from being weary of this terrible slavery that their lives then only begin to be irksome to them then sickness or age makes them incapable of taking pleasure in sin they desire to do. And are Satan and sin better masters than God and holiness? The latter, I am sure, even at present, are more good and kind to their servants. In keeping God's commandments, there is great reward, the Psalmist says. For God does not desire so to be trusted at all but that he will grant them so much in hands as may out-bid all that the devil or sin can bestow on them.

But then if we look beyond this life, and compare the infinite difference of the one and others to this time, one would think it is impossible that the devil and the flesh should so far prevail on rational beings as to detain them any longer with them. It does not need deliberation whether eternal happiness or eternal misery are to be preferred. Nothing but *not believing* of either one can make a person delay in his choice. Consider that little time that is to come, and how much of that little eating, drinking, sleeping and the necessities of the business of life will take from you and then judge you if you think you shall have more time allowed than what has been allotted to you. But if you either disbelieve what is spoken in the Scripture of another life, or imagine a very long stay in this life, saying your heart, with the evil servant, "My Lord delays in his coming," it is no wonder, then, if you begin to strike your fellow servants and to eat and drink with the drunkard. But a man must use great violence to his own understanding and conscience before he can arrive at such stupor of mind, and must think it is very much his interest to die like a beast, before he can believe that he shall do so.

Sermon 1: Coming to Christ in Haste

But all men under the Gospel's revelation are so far under the power of this truth, a life to come, that he cannot deny it, but his own fearful apprehensions will supply him with a lie about it. He looks out sometimes resting in his ease and security, and his is a fearful looking for of judgment and fiery indignation, while the man that has taken hold of this golden opportunity looks out as well, but his is looking for that blessed hope and the glorious appearing of the great God and his Savior. And can the sinner imagine his own day a far off, when he beholds the most youthful age, or the firmest state of health cannot secure him from its danger? There are a thousand accidents which we cannot foresee, and so not prevent, which may violently hurry us out of the world. The swallowing of a grape stone, or the cutting of a corn, have brought some people to their grave. We may stumble into it at a stone in the street, or a tile from a house may knock us down into the grave. The strongest man may be conquered by a fever in three or four days, or an apoplexy may dispatch him in so many hours or minutes. No one can tell where when, or by what instruments he shall pass out of this life. Which, if we consider, and also, that as the tree falls, so it lies; there is no rectifying the errors of our life after our death, but we shall forever continue in the state we die in. We must necessarily be very careful that death does not come on us unprepared. Solomon bid us, "Whatsoever our hand findeth to do, to do it with our might," for there is no work, nor device, nor knowledge, nor wisdom in the grave to which we will go. Now if this argument is pressing, as it is, that we ought therefore to lay hold of all opportunities for our souls while we live, because we can do nothing after we are dead; it may add to our seriousness to think, that it is uncertain whether a few days may not put an end to our life, and so to our working. It will be sad for the expiring soul to say, "Had I thought death had been so near, I would have given more heed to God's call to delaying sinners, that I might have been prepared for it." And yet his is the common case of the greatest part of mankind to set their last day at too great a distance from them.

To what has been said of the shortness of life, I might add the suddenness of Christ's coming to judgment. Yet a little while, and he that shall come, will come, and will not tarry. Now, since the Apostle's time, it is sixteen hundred years, and therefore, at this day we may well reckon of a little while; indeed it is true, "with God (as the Apostles expresses it) a thousand years are but as a day," and therefore, though it is a little while with God until our Lord comes, yet according to man's computation of time, it may be long according to that of our Savior, "Shall not God avenge his own Elect?" Though he bears with them long, I tell you, that he will avenge them speedily; but howsoever the term of "a little while" may be interpreted, we have certain tokens that his coming cannot be far off. St. Paul would not have the Thessalonians be troubled as if the Day of Christ were at hand, and the reason why it could not be so, he tells them, was, because that day should not come, except there came a falling away first, and that man of sin were revealed, the son of perdition whom Christ should destroy with the brightness of his coming. Now I think there is no Christian that doubts, but the artificial and

Sermon 1: Coming to Christ in Haste

profane spirit that is now in the world, speaks of him to be revealed, even that spirit that rules in the children of disobedience.

It would be a presumption to limit a time, seeing of that day and hour no man knows, so as to determine positively and precisely when it shall be. But, it would be a fool hardiness to be over confident, that it may not be even in our days. Whenever it is, it will certainly come unexpected of the greatest part of the world, even as a thief in the night. Our Savior's parable of the *Ten Virgins* may well instruct us what influence this day should have upon us. For when at midnight the Bridegroom came, the wise slumbered as well as the foolish, but their Lamps were burning, being furnished with oil, and therefore they went in with the Bridegroom to the marriage. Where, the foolish whose lamps were gone out, and their oil spent, had the door shut on them. From this he draws this exhortation, "Watch therefore, for you know neither the day nor the hour wherein the Son of Man cometh." They that shall be then alive, are likely to have no notice of it, nor shall they have any time to do anything towards their own salvation, for they shall be changed in a moment, in the twinkling of an eye, at the last trump. Alas for the fruitless wishes the delaying sinner shall then make, that he had worked while it was day; for now he sees an everlasting night approaching, in which he cannot work, but is to receive the reward of his sloth. Many times was he called on by the watchman to awake out of sleep, but he was still for a little while more desirous to slumber; and now that the last trumpet gives the alarm, he is raised indeed out of his sleep;

but before he can think to himself what to do, being filled with horror and despair, he is called on to give an account of what he has done. The surprise amazes him and puts him besides himself, puts him even before himself in such a way as to call to the mountains to hide him, as if they had ears to hear, or hearts to pity him; and the stones less rocky than his own heart, that would never relent at the most earnest imploring of God by the ministers of his word, and their calls to delaying sinners Alas! Now the sinner is diverted too much and taken up with other lovers, that the love of a Savior are not constraining, nor his mercies winning; but then his greatness will affright them, his terrors take hold, and his justice seize the sinner.

To prevent this state of the ungodly and impenitent, is the end of the ensuing sermons, which have the unhappiness to lack the author's own polishing, for which cause it is but justice, that what mistakes are found in them, may not be laid at the author's door, he being altogether ignorant of their Publishing, yet were they taken (as I am informed) by the pen of a ready writer, and one much acquainted with the author's preaching; and truly this just testimony cannot be denied to them, the spirit and lineaments of that worthy person, whose name they beat in the title is soundly on every word. He is a person whose name needs no *Encomiums*, having so many immortal tombs in the hearts of many of his hearers on whom his ministry has made such impressions, as no doubt will abide with them forever and carry the blessed effects into the other world.

Sermon 1: Coming to Christ in Haste

Reader, I shall not detain you longer on the porch, but only make these few requests to you. That you would read this small *call* over seriously, and with deliberation; and when you have done so, then seriously examine your own heart, and see if these things do not concern you. And that if you have any in your family that need an awakening call, that you would read either this or some other good book to them. That you make a due care and conscience of reading the holy Scriptures; of prayer both public and private; of hearing the word, and other ordinances commanded by God in the holy Scriptures. But above all, do not neglect to get a saving interest in Christ, concluding with this Scripture, Ezek. 33:11, "Say unto them, as I live, saith the Lord God, I have no pleasure in the death of the wicked; but that the wicked turn from his way and live. Turn ye, turn ye from your evil way; for why will ye die, O House of Israel?"

Sermon 1
Coming to Christ in Haste

Psalm 119:60, "I made haste, and delayed not to keep thy commandments."

To show you the coherence of these words with those that go before, I shall show you six things worthy of our imitation, which go *before* our text, but will bring us with haste *to* the text.

1. You have the wise choice that David made of God to be his portion. Verse 57, "Thou art my portion, O Lord." Some choose the world for their portion, some choose their pleasures for their portion; but alas these are but beggarly portions. David says very well let others make choice of what they will, I'll choose the blessed God, for my portion: I know that God will be a suitable portion, a durable portion, a sufficient and satisfying portion to me. And here he makes his appeal to God, "O Lord, thou art my portion."

2. You have David's fixed resolution on his choice, what he was resolved to do, "I have said that I will keep thy Word," in the same Verse.

3. You have David's supplication, his earnest prayer to God, that he might be enabled to perform his resolution, verse 58, "I entreated thy favor with my whole heart, be merciful unto me according to thy word," therefore, now, on my knees, I beg your grace, that I may perform your Word. He had resolved that he would keep the word of

God, and therefore he prays that God would help him to keep his word.

4. You have David's serious reflection on his ways and on his walks, verse 59, "I thought on my ways." How few scarcely do so much as seriously think on their ways, what they are doing, and where they are going? You think of the world, and you think of your sins, so as to gratify your lust, but when do you seriously think of your way, in order to turn to God?

5. You have David's resolution after he had thought on his ways; "I will keep thy word." I did wander, but I will not go on in my sin any longer; I thought on my ways, and turned my feet to your testimony.

6. You have David's putting into practice what before he resolved in the text, "I made haste, and delayed not to keep thy commandments."

Some men do not so much as resolve; some resolve, but do not pray; some do pray, but they do not consider, before and after prayer, where they have walked in the ways of God or not. Some do consider, but they do not turn; some do purpose to turn, but they delay. But, here is a copy for you all to walk after! "I delayed not to keep," *etc.* And so, we are come to the Text: The words are plain and easy. The *Doctrine* that I would speak to from them is this, "that what the blessed and eternal God commands us to do, is to be done with all possible speed, with all haste, without delay."

O! that you could say as David did, I have made haste, and have not delayed to keep your commandments!

A Call to Delaying Sinners

Listen, there is no room for delaying and trifling in the matters of your God, and in the concerns of your souls. If anything in the world requires haste, this does. I will give you four instances, and that everyone may take it as a pattern to copy.

The first is the instance of Abraham, Gen. 18, from the second verse to the eighth. There came three men to Abraham, that is, three angels in the shape of men, one of which was an *increased Angel,* the Blessed Son of God. They came to Abraham, and Abraham *made haste* to give entertainment to them, verse 6. Then he saw them, to meet them, and in verse 6 Abraham hastened into the tent of Sarah and said, "Make ready quickly." Listen, Jesus Christ that is preached to you, that is offered to you in the Gospel, O! where is the man that runs to meet with the blessed Christ! Oh, who is it that speaks to him, and says, "Make ready, Oh my soul, make ready quickly, and give the best room in your heart for this Christ that now stands before you at the door of your heart."

2. I would allude to the practice of the Israelites, that night they went out of Egypt, Exodus 12:11-12. "Ye shall eat it in haste," it is in the Lord's Passover. This is a figure of poor sinners being delivered by Christ out of worse than Egyptian bondage. Have you lived in a state of bondage so long, and God command you to come out, and will you not make haste? Exodus 12:33, "The Egyptians urged the people to send them out of the land in haste," for, they said, "We be all dead men." So, I say to you all, make haste and get out of your state of bondage, or else you will be so many dead men. Make note of my words, you will be

Sermon 1: Coming to Christ in Haste

so many damned souls. Luke 2:8-17, there, when they heard of Christ, that a Savior was born, that a Redeemer was come into the world, they said, "where is he?" And, when they were told, they made haste, and came and found our Savior, and Mary his mother in a manger, verse 16.

3. The third is that of Zachaeus, who when our Savior was passing by, ran up and climbed into the tree to see him. Our Savior looked up to him and said, "Zachaeus make haste and come down, for this day I must abide at thy house." And what did Zachaeus do? Did he linger, and say, afterwards it will be time enough? No, no; he made haste and came down, and received him joyfully.

4. A 4th instance is Mary, who, when she heard that Jesus was near, John 11:26-29, as soon as she heard that Christ had come, and that he called for her, arose quickly and came to him. But alas, the poor Ministers of Christ, they come one day after another to you, saying, listen, the Master is come, the Savior of souls is come; he alone that can redeem you from hell, is come and he calls for you. But, one delays, and another loiters. A third, a twentieth, a hundredth, they make nothing of all this but *delay*.

On this subject shall be shown some reasons; then the application; but the whole shall be to urge you to make speed and haste, to come to Christ. I shall give you five or six *reasons* why, that you should make all possible speed.

The things that God does command to you to do, and set about, require all possible speed, that they should be set on in haste without delay. Beloved hearers, do you think the great eternal God, speaks to you about toys and trifles? Surely you think that they are no better when you linger and loiter, one Sabbath after another, one month after another from year to year; you put off the work that God commands you to do, where there is nothing in this world that does so much concern you to do quickly, and with haste, and with speed. Let me entreat you, and implore you, for God's sake, seriously to weigh what are the commands of the glorious God on you; then tell me if they do not require all possible speed. Here are six things under this head.

1. The dreadful God commands you, sinner, to repent of your sin, and tells you "Thou art damned" if you do not do them. And will you still delay and loiter, and linger, and not make haste? Beloved hearers, you will find it true, that "except ye repent," and that soon too, your souls will be damned. Now consider, sinner, must your soul be forever damned and tormented in the Lake of burning brimstone and that forever, except you would repent, and will you yet delay? Will you make haste to repent, and today! Ah beloved, is there room for dallying, to put off this work of repentance, where God commands you? Will you put it off for another year still, and another month, when the blessed God assures you that if you die without repentance, you are lost forever. Shall not the gate of heaven be shut against your soul when you die, except you repent while you live? And yet, will you linger? Turn and see what Christ says, Luke 13:3, "Except ye repent, ye shall all likewise perish." Do you think that Christ speaks unadvisedly to you? For, he says again, verse 5, "Except ye repent, ye shall surely perish."

Sermon 1: Coming to Christ in Haste

2. You are commanded by God to make your peace with him. This work lies in your hand, and is yet undone by many of you, and will you still delay? Will you not make haste, as it is the time to make your peace with God? O! do it quickly, with all possible speed. For if you do not make your peace with God quickly, God and your soul will be enemies forever. You were born an enemy to God, and if you do not make your peace with God, you will die an enemy to God. O! that you would believe these words, as you will shortly find them true, you would no longer doubt. But you would now make haste to make your peace with God. Poor sinner! How can you sleep, and eat, and drink in peace, while your peace is not yet made to your God! What do you think you poor delaying trifler? Can you make your part good with God? Can you resist Almighty Power? Was there ever a man since the creation of the world that hardened his heart against God and prospered? And do you think that you can do more, than all the men since the world was created could ever do? Come, I will give you a way to have some character in this. If you can stand up, come forth, and buckle on your armor, rouse up yourself, and play the man. If God afflicts you, do not flinch, do not crouch to him, and run under the sheets of your bed. If God afflicts you with the gout, gallstones, or a virus, or if you are sick at heart, do not cry out. What, a stout-hearted sinner cry out, when God does but lay his finger on you? When God shall commission you to the grave, say, "Lord, I will not die!" And make your words good if you can. When God shall sentence you to hell, say, "Lord, I will not be damned," and make your words good if

you can. When God gives devils a commission to drag you to hell, say to God and the devils, that you will not go. Ah, poor sinner! Will you in this way stand against this God, that can turn you into hell, and into torments; and will you yet delay, and not make haste to make your peace with God! Rather take the advice of Christ, Luke 14:31-32. "What king goeth to make war against another King, and sitteth not down first and consulteth, whether with ten thousand, he is able to meet him that cometh against him with twenty thousand?" Ah, so do you, beloved! Consider, whether you are able to stand with Almighty strength! And if you are not, send up your prayers to heaven; and desire that God would be at peace with you.

  3. This work lies on your hand, to get pardon of your sins. To get off the guilt that lies on your soul. And this requires haste; quickly, or not at all. Are you not a sinner? Do you not have a multitude of sins? And are not your sins heinous? Are you not guilty of many sins of omission? Have you been always accustomed to pray? Would to God you had. Have you always been accustomed to walk closely with God? I wish you had. O! what have you omitted to do that God has command of you? Are you not guilty of many sins of commission; that God charged you on pain of death to do? Say yes, or no. If you say no, your very tongue proves you to be liar. O! then make haste to Christ! Besides, are you not guilty of great and heinous sins? Have you not sinned against knowledge and conscience? Against Law and Gospel? Have you not sinned against the mercy and patience of God? How many oaths have you sworn? How many times have you been naughty?

Sermon 1: Coming to Christ in Haste

How many times have you been drunk? How many Sabbaths have you misspent? How many sermons have you slighted? Sinner, tell me, can you hear the punishment that God will inflict on you for these sins, unless you speedily will return to God? Listen, I wonder in my heart! I wonder how you can sleep all night and not dream of hell! How do you sleep securely, and not dream of being damned when you lie down with the guilt of so many sins on your souls, and not one pardoned, and not one forgiven! I wonder how you can drink and be entertained, and be so merry in your life when your sins are not yet forgiven of you!

4. The eternal God commands you, on the pain of damnation, to hasten to come to Christ, to come away to Christ, and come to him on the Gospel's terms. Does not this require haste? Is here room for delaying! For God's sake, beloved, consider, you are damned if you do not believe on Christ. Yet will you delay and stand trifling with the eternal God, whether you shall believe or not! 1 John 3:23, "And this is his commandment, that we should believe on the name of the Son of God." Oh, why do you not haste, and not delay to do this command of God? See how strictly God charges this on your souls, that if you do not believe, you must be damned. For, "he that believeth not shall be damned," (Mark 16:16). Is there any room for trifling? Is there any time to delay, while you are in danger of damnation, as long as you do not believe! The wrath of God abides on thee, while you do not believe in Jesus Christ. John 3:36, "But he that believeth not, the wrath of God abideth on him." And is this an ease to be delaying in! Sinner what if you had great riches? What if you had great

riches and did not have Christ? What, though you have made haste to get an estate and home? What is that without Christ? What is this without sanctifying grace? What if you had all the pleasures that the world can afford? If you have all that your heart can desire, and not have Christ, you are miserable. Sinner, remember, it is not riches but Christ that must save and keep you out of hell! Without Christ there is no peace. Without Christ there is no pardon! Without Christ there is no escaping the damnation of hell! Without Christ there is no entering into heaven! And will you yet delay!

5. You have death and judgment to prepare for, and does not this require haste? Will you yet dally, and delay and not with all possible speed endeavor to be found in careful preparation of death and judgment! Tell me, are you prepared to die, if death should seize you this night? Are you prepared to die? How many of you if you were on your sick beds, that conscience would tell you, "You are not prepared to die!" No. What, and yet you sit still! O! what makes you so sick to do that sinner! When do you not see that you are so near to another world! Are you prepared to leave this world, yet you never repented from your sins? Are you prepared to die, to go down to your grave, yet never to heartily beg for Christ and his grace? Are you prepared to die while you sit in the gall of bitterness, and bond of iniquity? While you are a stranger to God and Christ, and grace, you are not fit to die. What, and will you yet sit still, as if past all danger? Or else can you put away the striking of death by force? O! that you would see what reason there is to make haste, and not to delay. 2 Peter 3:12,

"Looking for and hastening to the coming of the day of the Lord." Make note of that, you should be hastening for the coming of the day of the Lord. Do you hasten for the coming of this day? Will you sit still and not make your peace with God? The day of reckoning is coming and all things will be set straight between God and your souls; and will you delay, and not make haste?

6. And lastly, you are yet uncertain whether you shall be damned or saved. And does not this require all possible need? Does not this call for all the haste which you can make to get an assurance of the love of God, and of salvation after death? How soon you may be on a death bed, you don't know. Now, suppose you were dying, and think, "O, I must bid farewell to all my friends! I must leave my husband, and wife, children, brothers, sisters, friends, and neighbors. I must die, but where I go next, I cannot tell! There are but two places to receive souls after death, heaven and hell; but which of these must I go to, I do not know." Not know? And yet you still sit and delay. When the blessed God has commanded you to make all diligence to make your calling and election sure you delay? Is this diligence, to not even think about it one year after another? Is this your diligence that you use? Put this question to your soul, "What will become of it when you leave this world?" For God's sake arise make haste, sinner, make haste, lest you be shut out of Christ's kingdom, which you take no care to make sure of.

That is the first reason or general head, why the command of God should be set about with all speed without delay; "that what the blessed and eternal God commands us to do, is to be done with all possible speed, with all haste, without delay."

Sermon 2
Now or Never

Psalm 119:60, "I made haste, and delayed not to keep thy commandments."

In our last sermon we considered making haste to come to Christ, considered from Psalm 119:60 where David expresses that whatsoever God commands he will do speedily; that what the blessed and eternal God commands us to do, is to be done with all possible speed, with all haste, and *without* delay.

Beloved, make haste; make haste, and do not delay any longer; for all the time that is before you is little enough for you to do what God commands you. He that begins his obedience to God's commands soonest, or at least in his youth, will have a *little time enough* to do what God commands. You that are older, if you had begun to work as soon as you began to understand things, you would have found plenty of time enough to have done any work, even if you lived a thousand years in this world. But, being you have a little time to live which is left, must not this little time be little enough for you to do the work that God set you in the world to do? Do you have one day to spare, or one hour to spare? O! how many of this world spend their time so as if they had time too much and work too little! When, God knows, your time is of the least.

There are these five things more under this head, which will press you to *make haste,* not to delay one hour

A Call to Delaying Sinners

longer. O! could I but prevail with one sinner resolvedly to go home, and to say, "I will delay no longer, I will make haste to keep the commandments of my God!" Consider *here:*

1. You have a great work to do, and therefore should not lose one minute of time to do it. You have many strong lusts to overcome. Many temptations to resist. Many duties to perform. You have the knowledge of God and Christ to get, and of your own heart, the knowledge of your state now, and of your eternal state hereafter. You have many prayers to make, many hours to be spent in searching your heart, and examining your state. And is not all the time that you have before you if you were to begin today, little enough to do this great work that God lays on you to do?

2. The work enjoined by God, it is difficult work, and hard work too. The more difficult your work is, if you are wise, the more time you will take to do it. Is not to set your heart and your love on God, to love him above all, and to please him before all, is this not a hard and difficult work, do you think, when the heart of a sinner naturally loves *anything* better than God? To have your will to bow to Christ, and submit to Christ, and receive of Christ, when it is rebellious and stubborn? Is not this hard work, to change your heart, to break your hard and stony heart? To reform your life, is not this a hard and difficult work? And yet, all this is commanded by God. You say, this work is not so hard. If this work is not hard, why is it not done? If it is hard, why do you not go diligently about it? Consider then that it is difficult work that you have to do.

Sermon 3: Repent Today

3. The work that you have to do, in light of another world that is eternal, is a *necessary* work. It is work that must be done, or your soul will be undone, and that forever. And will you yet delay, and will you yet stand dallying, and putting it off, whether you should best do it or not! If the work were indifferent, whether to be done, or left undone, I would not blame you for making no more haste in it; but this is not the case. This work is more necessary than food when you are hungry, more necessary than medicine, when you are sick. Beloved people, you must be holy, or you must never see God, except that you shall see him as your eternal terror. You must turn from sin, or burn in hell! You must repent, or you cannot be saved. There is such a great necessity for doing this work, that God *commands* you to do it. Is it an indifferent thing, whether you escape the damnation of hell, or not! If not, behold, holiness is the way to heaven! Faith in Christ is the way to heaven! This must be done, or your soul must not be saved. Beloved, if there is any business in this world, that lies on our hands that is necessary to be done, *this is it.*

4. This work that God commands you to do, it is a soul-work. And I am sure that such a soul work as this should not be delayed. Soul-work should be done with all possible speed. O! that you would resolve and say, "It is my soul that must be dammed or saved; therefore, I will make haste! It is my soul that must go to heaven or hell, therefore, I will make haste to look after the salvation of my soul." You have but one soul; only one soul. Will you make haste to feed your body when it is hungry? Will you make haste

to quench your thirst when it is dry? And to send for a doctor, when you are in danger of death, and to cry out to those about you, "Oh do not stay here," you tell them, "make haste, bring in the doctor quickly," and yet in the meantime you never think of your soul? Is your body better than your soul? Is not your soul far better? Will you take care to feed and clothe the body, and delay getting an interest in Christ to save your soul? Why are you so careful for a dying body, that within a little while shall be nothing but a lump of lifeless dust? You don't know that not long from now, possibly, men shall carry your bodies on their shoulders to the grave, and lay them in the dust, and there they will rot. What? Will you take such care to make provision for a corruptible body, and yet neglect your souls! What are you thinking friends? What do you mean by doing that? What ails men that they delay in this way with themselves? Are they not *out of their minds?*

5. And lastly, if you think nothing that has been said is worth regarding, yet I pray that you consider the work that God commands you to mind in this world, for it is a work for eternity! And will you put it off for another year, month, or week! Do you all think that a short life on earth is not a little time enough to prepare for an eternal life, for an endless eternity! Are a few years too much to be spent with all diligence, that you may be ready for an everlasting state, to which you are a hastening to? Beloved hearers, you and I are all before God this day, but how soon, we may be in an unalterable estate is unknown to us; you are now in time, tomorrow you may be in eternity. You

may be in an everlasting state. What, and yet make no more haste! Death is at your backs, heaven and hell are before you. And what! And yet delay? What! At the brink of an everlasting state, and to make no more haste to do what God has commanded you! Remember man, remember, it is heaven that must be lost or won forever! It is eternal joy, that you must have, or go without whenever you shall leave this world! It is *everlasting* torments or *everlasting* blessedness that you must enter into, when you leave this world. Yet will you not make haste to do that work, that God commands you to do! Arise sinner in the name of God, awake, be *up and doing*, if you love your soul. Make haste, sinner, make haste, begin today, before tomorrow. Begin this hour, before the next, to do the work that God commands you; for all the time that is before you, is little enough to do it in.

Consider this work, beloved, that God commands you to do, must be done *now, or never.* What, and yet sit still, and yet delay! It must be now, or never. Friends, if you will repent, you must now repent, or never to any purpose. If you will make your peace with God, it must be done now or never! God has set in this world to make preparation for another. God has set us in this life, that we may make ready for another. We are in this world *on trial,* and accordingly, as we behave ourselves and mind our work, or let it alone, so it must be with us forever. This world is the place, this life the time, when work for heaven must be done or never be done. "Whatsoever thy hand findeth to do, do it with all thy might, for there is no work, nor device, nor knowledge, nor wisdom in the grave, whither thou goest," (Eccl. 9:10).

O! that every trifler in the matters of his God, and of his soul, would write that verse on his bedroom door. In this you must mind these three *things:*

First it is plainly said, that you are going to your grave; you are on your journey to your grave. You are on your way to the dust. Whether you are sleeping or waking, you are going to your grave. Whether working or playing you are going to your grave. Whether drinking or playing sports, you are going to your grave. In this journey you never stand still. The child is going to its grave as soon as it is born.

2. In the grave there is no work to be done; no preaching there, nor any means nor helps there. I'll speak about this more at a later time.

3. Therefore it follows, that what you now have to do, it should be done with all your might, and with all haste and possible speed. What you have in your hand to do, do it with all your might, for there is no work to do in the grave to which you are going. Jesus Christ worked all the more because his time was but short. He said, "I must work the work of him that sent me, while it is day; for the night cometh wherein no man can work." Behold your day is passing away! The night is coming on! Oh, do your work while the day lasts, for when the night comes no man can work. You must repent savingly now, or never! You must believe on Christ now, or never! You must be made holy and become the children of God now, or never! Oh, I think these words, "now or never" should alarm the most drowsy sinner! But to set this home, that what God commands

Sermon 3: Repent Today

must be done now, or never, I will lay before you these seven things.

1. After death there shall be no offers of mercy, nor tenders of pardon into all eternity. Therefore, now or never. You must now do what God commands, or not at all. *Now* God calls you and Christ calls you, and the Spirit calls you, and ministers call you, that you would leave off your sin. But if you stop up your ears and harden your heart until death, after death none of these shall call to you into forever! God never says to damned souls, "What do you say now, will you receive mercy now, will you have a Savior now, and listen to me now?" No, God never took this course as yet, and God will never do that.

2. After death there is no repentance or believing; therefore, this must be done now, or never. When death has shut your eyes, and separated your soul from your body, if you die an unbeliever, you shall never afterwards have faith. If you die impenitent, you shall never afterwards repent. Possibly, damned souls may repent in hell where they did not repent on earth. But, repentance in hell is only an aggravation of their misery, it being fruitless repentance without the Spirit. What, do you think those that would never be good while they lived, will be good in hell! It is true, there are many sins that men commit on earth, that they shall not commit in hell. The drunkard there shall not be drunk anymore. The gambler there shall have no more games to play. Therefore, now, or never.

3. The soul after death enters into an everlasting state, where there shall be no alteration forever; therefore, what you do for your souls, must be done now, or never.

The soul, when it goes into another world, wherever it first takes its lodgings, it will be forever. There once damned, and forever damned! Once in hell, and forever there; therefore, it must be now, or never. If a man in an unconverted state should die today, and news is brought to you tomorrow, what has become of his soul? The news would be, such a one is dead, and damned too. Yes, you see, the soul enters into an everlasting state. Luke 16:22-23, there Lazarus died, and his soul went unto unalterable joys. The rich man died, and his soul went to unchangeable torments. When a man dies, he goes to his place. Every soul has a place he must go to when he leaves the body, Acts 1:25. Judas died and went to "his own place." Hell is the unbelievers own place.

4. When a man dies, wrath and justice take their turns, and while a man lives, mercy and patience take their turns. Beloved hearers, the attributes of God, as I may so speak, take their turns now; mercy and patience take their turns. Mercy takes its turn, and says, "sinner, you are undone. Here is a Christ for you. You are miserable, come to me, and I will help you." This is Mercy's turn, but the soul does not yet regard it. Therefore, patience takes its turn, and says, "until the next Lord's Day." It may be, the sinner will be wise then. If not, it takes another turn with him. The sinner might think to himself that God is very patient with him not repenting, and it may be, Patience waits from one year, to another; from ten years to another ten years. Yet, the sinner does not hear nor regard Mercy. Then, when the soul is separated from the body, wrath and justice take their turns. Then Mercy says, "Lord, I delivered

to this man the Christ, even as long as he lived, but he refused." And Patience says, "I was patient with the sinner in his life, and waited on him, even now to his last gasp." "Therefore, now we Mercy and Patience deliver him up to the hands of Wrath and Justice; take him. We Mercy and Patience are done with this man's soul forever."

5. Stay a little longer in your sins, until death has closed your eyes, then the cries and calls, and importunities for Mercy shall never be heard. God will then become a God not to be intreated. Now, if you beg for Mercy, you may have it. If you beg and cry, and call for pardon to God, on the conditions of the Gospel of Jesus Christ, and believe on God's Christ, you may have mercy; but refuse a little longer, then if you cry to all eternity your cries shall never be heard, nor regarded. See this where Christ says in Matt. 7:21-22ff, *etc.* where men say to him "Lord, Lord," and where he says back to them, "No, I never knew you." No, Christ says, "I know you not whence ye are," (Luke 13:25). See there the strong cries that men shall make, and all in vain. In Luke 16:26 what strong requests did the rich man give while he was in hell, and still all of it was denied to him. Should he then beg for the least mercy, as much as one drop of water, it could not be had by him.

6. What God commands, it must be done now, or never, because when once time has come and gone, it then will never be gained back. The last Lord's Day will never come again. Sinner, the time that you should have prayed, but did not, will never come again. All that you can give, will not buy back one hour again. And when you are dead and gone out of this world, God will never trust you with

one more day, to do that which you did not do while in this world. God will not say to a damned soul in hell, here was a fooling and a delaying sinner, that delayed to come to God while on earth, that made no haste to come to Christ, while Christ might have been had. God will not then say to them, "Come, go your way again. I will release you for a little while; go and sit under the same minister again, I will try you out for another life." O! friends, this will never be! Therefore, it is *now, or never.* Job 7:6, "My days are swifter than a weaver's shuttle, and are spent without hope. The eye of him that seeth me, shall see me no more," *etc.* Friends, it is not long that you shall dwell in your houses, and lodge in your beds. Death will quickly come and haul you out, and take you out of this world, and you must never come again. Job 14:7, "There is hope of a tree: if it be cut down, that it will sprout again, but man dieth and wasteth away." Yes, man dies wherever he is! Verse 12, "So man lieth down, and rises not again, until the world vanish away." If a man die shall he live again? *i.e.* shall he live on earth again? Shall he come and sit under the means of grace again? No. Heb 9:27, "It is appointed for all men once to die." Make note of this, a man shall die but once a natural death. The soul is but once to be separated from the body. It is appointed for all men once to die. Oh Lord, how well should all the work that is to be done, that must be done but once! Must you die but once! O! then how *carefully* should that work be done!

7. After death is the time of receiving your wages of reward; therefore, your work must be done now, or never. If your work is done, you go away to heaven, if it is not

Sermon 3: Repent Today

done, you go away down to hell. Immediately after death, the reward is given, or the punishment is inflicted. When the servant of the laboring man is to be reckoned with at night, if his work is not done, can he expect a reward? Can you look for heaven when you have not believed, not repented, not closed with Jesus Christ on Gospel terms? So, when the Day of Judgment comes presently after death, you have sowed certain things, and can you expect to reap eternal life? Or shall that be your sowing time, that should have been your reaping time? Friends, this is now your sowing time, your praying time, and your repenting time; therefore, do it now without delay, for this must be done *now or never.* Consider, all of you, you must make haste, there is no room for delay, for what God commands you to do, it must be done, *now or never.*

Sermon 3
Repent Today

Psalm 119:60, "I made haste, and delayed not to keep thy commandments."

In our last sermon we considered doing what God commands now, or never, considered from Psalm 119:60.

So, God commands you to act without delay, to yield obedience to his commands. The time is set and commanded by God, as well as the work of any duty itself. God does not only tell you *what* to do, but he tells you *when* you are to do it. We consider in this sermon, the time, as it relates to *today*.

The same God, sinner, that commands you to repent, commands you to repent *today*. The same God that commands you to believe and receive his Son, commands you to do it now at this very instant. The same God that commands you to leave your sin, and turn to him, commands you to do it now, *without delay*. Where does God give liberty to any man, to put off his repentance until tomorrow? Show me the place if you can in his word? Much less, until you are a man, much less, until you are old; yet this is in the thoughts and hearts of too many people. "Do not repent just yet," is the voice of the devil, and not of God. "Let holiness alone for now," this is the language of your enemy, and of your cursed and corrupted heart. It is not the voice of God. Where does God say that he allows you to spend this day in a natural state? In what chapter, or what verse is it, that God gives you space to reject Christ for one hour, and to neglect God and your soul for one hour? Show me the place if you can. Let God alone, and Christ alone, if you can show me. Do it so long as you have leave from God so to do. No, but this you cannot do. Will the blessed and holy God give you time to rebel against him? For one day will he give you leave to do so? No; but I can show you, sinner, one place after another, where God commands your speedy return. Eccl. 12:1, "Remember thy Creator in the days of thy youth." Remember him. Remember what to do; to obey his commandments, to fear him. Remember him, to love him. Remember him, to make a speedy and voluntary resignation of your souls to him. Observe in that verse it is not only said, "Remember thy Creator in the days of thy youth." So, you young ones perhaps may say, "you do," and yet stay longer, yet a year or two; but make note of this, there is one word more, "Remember *now* thy Creator in the days of thy youth." 2 Cor. 6:2, "Now is the appointed time: now is the day of salvation." Friends, there is not one of you all that can say "tomorrow is the day of salvation," or the next week, or the next year shall be the day of salvation. Matthew 6:33, "Seek ye *first* the Kingdom of God and the righteousness thereof." How contrary is the commandment of God to the practice of men? First for an estate, then for holiness, as I was told, was a saying of one that I was lately with, that lies under a horrible distress of his soul. He was very eager to get an estate, quickly; fame and fortune, and yet, after he had done this he cried, "God forgive me," Heb 3:7-8, "Wherefore as the Holy Ghost saith, Today if ye will hear his voice, harden not your hearts, as in the provocation, in the day of temptation in the wilderness." Heb. 4:7, again, he limits a certain day, saying, "today if you will hear his voice, harden not your hearts." Now seriously ponder this, then tell me. Is there any room in your delays?

5. The last reason is this, there is no room for your deliberation in this cause, whether you will obey the commands of God or not, and consequently there can be no room for delay. There is no time to be spent, to think whether you should keep God's command or not. There are some things that do not come under men's deliberation, to spend any time to deliberate whether we are to do them or not.

As for instance, which of you deliberate whether you shall eat or drink or not? No man would, but for quantity or quality, you may deliberate, but whether to eat or drink at all, you must not deliberate or you starve and die. So, the ultimate end of man does not come under man's deliberation. No man deliberates whether he shall be happy or not at the end. Now, such is your obedience to the commandments of God. Doing that which he commands you to do, will you spend time to deliberate whether the blessed God should be beloved or not? Will you spend time to deliberate whether the blessed Savior shall be believed on or not? No, there is no room or deliberation in this case. No man will have the face to dare to call these things into question. Now is there no room for deliberation; yet, is there room for your delay?

So much for the reasons here; now I will turn to some application of the doctrine. And there is but one main *use* that I intend to speak about on this subject, that is a *Use of Exhortation*.

Must the commandments of God be kept without delays, with all earnest haste and possible speed? Oh, then beloved hearers, be exhorted in the fear of God, without delay, to set about the work that God commands you to do. Come, begin this day before tomorrow. O! come for God's sake be persuaded to begin this work, this very hour before the next hour comes around. Sinner, leave your sins, just now, for the eternal God commands you to do so; forsake your wickedness just now, for the blessed and glorious God gives you charge to do so. Turn to God, believe in Christ, just now without delay. Oh, that I could but persuade you, to look about you, to be *up and doing*. If anything in this world requires *haste,* this does. For your soul's sake arise, and be up and doing. If the devil tempts you to delay, do not listen to him, but say, "The eternal God commands me now to repent and turn to Christ, and the safety of my soul work requires that I should do it with all possible speed." If your companions suggest to you, there is time enough yet, then reply and say, "Oh that is not true, the eternal God requires me presently to leave my sins." If your own corrupt and slothful heart should say the same, Oh, it is not true, the eternal God requires me to make haste, and the safety of my soul requires me to do this as well. Oh, you young men, consider earnestly that you may not live until you are old. You young children, that understand what I say, make haste, for you may die while you are young. You old gray headed sinner, make haste and do not delay, for your time is almost already spent.

A Call to Delaying Sinners

To force this exhortation, I shall urge it with ten arguments.

1. The danger and the miserable state that your soul is in, while you are unconverted, requires you to make haste. Your natural state is wretched, your condition deplorable. Oh, why do you not make haste to get out of that condition? Dangers seen and apprehended usually speed up to hastening. Tell me, sinner, if a bear were right behind you chasing you down, or a lion was at your back, what haste would you make to get away from them, so that you are not torn in pieces? If you were in a wild and desolate wilderness, that is full of pits and serpents, and wild beasts, and night were coming on you, what haste would you make to get out of it? If you were in your bed, and at midnight you heard a voice, "Get up, awake, your house is on fire," would you not make haste? Would you say, "There is no need of haste," and turn and fall back to sleep again, and take another nap in your bed? Behold, your danger is a million times more, while in your sin. Is your soul not better than your body? Is not your soul better than your possessions? And would you rise in haste to your body and your goods, and will not make haste to save your soul, and that from hell's flames! Or will you turn yourself like a sluggard on the bed of carnal security, and say, "Let me alone, do not disturb me, there is no such haste." In Genesis 19:15-16, and the verses following, Sodom was to be burnt with fire, and the people that were in the city only God could have mercy on, and Lot was there, and some with him, therefore the angel came to hasten him, "to get away," because of this danger. This applies, sinner, to those

of you who are in a natural state, in danger of a worse fire than that of Sodom. And God commends you to make haste lest you are consumed. But still, you linger and loiter, and God sends to you again, saying, "Sinner, escape for your life, for your soul, do not look behind you, after the world, and after your sins, and lusts. Make haste, for it is your life." When David was in danger of being seized on by Saul, he made great haste to get out of that danger, for Jonathan, his friend, had given him a sign, by shooting an arrow. He spoke to David in the arrow shot, that David would know whether it was good or evil that was appointed for him, "And Jonathan cried after the lad, Make speed, haste, stay not. And Jonathan's lad gathered up the arrows, and came to his master. But the lad knew not any thing: only Jonathan and David knew the matter," (1 Sam. 20:38-39). Ah, you see! Yet you say, sinner, I will have fun, I will spend money, I will do what I want, even though your case is very dangerous. Saul, when he was in danger, the Philistines invaded the land, but he got away in haste. When David was coming against Nabal's, house, Abigail made haste to pacify and turn away his anger. But alas, what was the danger of Lot to your danger! Or the danger of David, of Saul, or of Nabal's house to the danger you are in.

  First of all, will you delay to make haste to the commandments of God? God himself is your enemy. There is enmity between God and your soul. Know then, while you are trifling, God is angry with you. The eternal God is provoked by your rebellion against his Law. And is this a state to be delayed in? If a great man was your enemy, what haste would you make to be reconciled to him? If a man on whom is your dependence and livelihood, should become your enemy, Oh, how would you try to get his favor again! Would not the thoughts of his displeasure awaken you out of your sleep! Psa. 7:11, "God is angry with the wicked every day." Make note of this, God is daily angry with you, while a wicked man. Will you break God's commandments? And is this a condition to be continued in, when God is angry with you every day? God is angry with the wicked every day in the week, every day in the year. Verse 12, "If he turn not, he will whet his sword, he hath bent his bow, and made it ready. He hath also prepared for him the instruments of death." Think it through, the angry God has taken his bow in his hand, yes, he has strung and bent his bow and he has taken his arrow out of the quiver, and put it to the string, and drawn it back to the top; and sinner, if you are the target that God aims at, if you are the bullseye, he will shoot his arrow in fury, so that it shall strike you to the very heart, and who shall heal that wound! Tell me now, is this a state you want to continue in? Oh, it is, because you do not know what God's anger is! Could you speak with devils, if they would speak plainly with you? They could tell you what God's anger is. If you could speak with a damned soul, they could tell you what God's anger is. Oh, if you knew and considered, what God's anger is you would say, "Oh this is not a state for me to abide in a day longer."

  Take these six properties where God is your enemy.

Sermon 3: Repent Today

First of all, this angry God is omnipotent. Do you have almighty power? Behold, he makes the mountains to smoke, and the earth, and devils to tremble. This, sinner, is he that is angry with you every day.

Secondly, this God is omniscient, and you cannot deceive him as to make him believe, *you* are *his* friend, who are indeed not.

Thirdly, this God that is angry with you every day, is an omnipresent God. And then in your distress, will you hasten to him? Consider, you that will not hasten to him, whether you can hasten *from* him? You that will not hasten to him, to a holy submission, and a voluntary resignation of yourselves to God, whether you hasten from him, trying to run away.

Fourthly, he is a righteous God that is angry with you every day. You cannot bribe him with your gifts. Your silver and your gold he will hate.

Fifthly, he is eternal too, and will never die. Behold this God that is angry every day with you, shall never die. If a man were your enemy, you may die, or else he may die, so you may be delivered from his anger. But this is not the case between God and your soul. God ever lives to take vengeance on you. He lives to all eternity, to punish you into eternity. To punish you for sinning against him. And even when you die, this does not deliver you from the angry God. No, but it is that you die, and then fall directly into his hands.

Sixthly, and lastly, this God that is angry with you every day, with whom you delay, is an unchangeable God. He will never change to be a friend to you, except you change, to become an obedient subject to him, and yield obedience to his commands.

Will you delay to keep the commandments of God, well, then, you are as very near relation to the devil. The devil is your father all this while, and you are his servant and his child. And to you that say you defy the devil and all his works, why then do you yet delay to leave his service and work? What do you think, is this relation to the devil so honorable, and is his work so delightful, and will his wages be so desirable that you so hate to leave him and turn to God? This is certainly true, that there is this relation and nearness between the devil and a wicked man. See Acts 13:10, where the Apostle says of a wicked man, "Thou enemy of all righteousness, thou child of the devil." Consider, you that are children of the devil, can be made the children of God, and will you not make haste to have this done? What if God should say to you at last, "You who are in a relationship as a child of the devil, and have him to be your father, and remain there, go down, go to your father the devil in hell, and you shall have a whole eternity to be there with him."

3. All the while you delay, you are under all the curses of the Bible; you are liable to all the punishments and threatenings in Scripture, and God may without delay inflict them all on you, you who delay to come to him. Gal. 3:10, "Cursed is he that coutinueth not in all things that are written in the Book of the Law to do them." You have not continued to do so much as *one thing* written in the Law. Oh, then, if God shall curse you, who shall bless you? Sinner, did you ever read this Bible; or if you have perused

this book, have you not seen the threatenings of God against graceless men, and ungodly men, and delaying sinners? Or, do you despise those sayings, and not make haste to get out of that condition in which you are exposed to God's wrath?

4. While you delay to keep the commandments of God, you are under the sentence of the Gospel as well. Ah beloved, if the Gospel condemns you, where are you going to appeal to? I'm not saying that at this time this sentence is a final sentence. No, until your unbelief is final this sentence against you is not final. Sinner, come, believe quickly, or else your unbelief *will be* a final unbelief; then this sentence of the Gospel, will be a final sentence too. The Gospel has its threatenings as well as the Law, yes, and even more severe ones as well. You that are ready to say, "You preachers are too sharp in your preaching when you give us nothing but hell and damnation." I speak no more than I find in the Gospel itself; and that Christ has spoken himself. Do you think that we are too sharp, and too hard in our sermons? You can cast that reproach on God that tells us what we are to tell you. We do not do any more but tell you what this God says, and what you must expect, and where you must shortly be, if you do not make haste and come away to Christ. Remember, Mark 16:16, "He that believeth not shall be condemned." This is Christ himself that shall judge you shortly that tells you this. John 3:36, "He that believeth not on the Son of God, the wrath of God abides on him." Heb. 2:3, "How shall we escape if we neglect so great a salvation!" Matthew 18:3, "Verily, verily I say unto you, except ye be converted, ye cannot

enter into the Kingdom of God." Luke 13, "Except ye repent ye shall all like wise perish." Heb. 2:4, "Without Holiness no man shall see the Lord." Now, what do you all say to these? Do we speak more than God speaks? Or have we said more than God himself has said? If you cannot bear this doctrine, tell me; why were you not one of God's counselors, and why didn't you advise and direct your Maker, to make better Laws, and better terms for sinners, than in the Gospel which he has done? Should your Maker ask *you* on what terms and conditions you would be saved? You must take *his terms*, or you will not be saved at all. John 3:18, "He that believeth not, is condemned already." Make note of the sentence, "He that does not believe." Ah poor sinner, you are a condemned man, yet will you not make haste, and will you sit still? And will you not come and beg of God that you would be pardoned?

5. All this while that you do delay, all your sins stand uncrossed in the Book of God; and is this a safe condition to be continued in? How many oaths, sinner, have you sworn! How many Holy Sabbaths have you profaned! How many times have you derided godliness? How many hundred times have you neglected to pray? To call on God? How many lies have you told, and not one of them forgiven! Poor delaying trifler? Do you not know, that you must be either pardoned or condemned? And you cannot be pardoned while you are unsanctified and unconverted to Jesus Christ. O! what will you do when you leave this world, and stand in judgment, and God shows you the book of knowledge, and you find all your sins have not been crossed out in his book but stand ready?

Sermon 3: Repent Today

6. While you delay to keep the commandments of God you are in daily danger of damnation. Friends, are you not reasonable creatures? Do you sit unmoved under the plain preaching of the word? But if those things are true, as you will certainly know and find them to be, why do you still delay and not strive to make more a hastening effort to get out of the condition which exposes you to so much eternal damnation? If the Word of God is so dreadful, what do you think the damnation itself will be like? Yet this is your danger while you delay to keep the commandments of your God. What are you in danger of? In danger of a place of utter darkness. In danger of a bottomless pit? In danger of a place of torment? In danger of a burning fiery furnace? In danger of a place of continual torment with fire, and with brimstone. Sinner, when you lie down, you are in danger of hell, and how do you know whether you will wake up before you are in hell? Sinner, consider how dangerous you sleep when you go to bed. Who dares to assure you that you will not be in hell before the sun rises again? Where is it that you can delay and sit at your dinner table and ponder and think about that judgment hour, and say to yourself, "now I am past danger of being damned. Now, I have a promise from God that my soul shall not be cast into hell." Friend, what do you mean by thinking in that way! Beloved people, what do you think on! How do you hear this and not be concerned! How can you eat and drink, and sleep as if you were not in danger of hell! Can you bear the wrath of God, the torments of the damned! Can you endure it? If you can, then let Christ alone! But I say, to speak about the torments of hell, is something

altogether different than to literally be in them, which you cannot imagine.

O! friends, listen to this counsel, from one that earnestly desires the salvation of your souls. For God commands you to act without delay *today*, to yield obedience to all his commands.

Sermon 4
Stop Your Sinning

Psalm 119:60, "I made haste, and delayed not to keep thy commandments."

We considered, in the last sermon, that God commands you to act without delay, to yield obedience to all his commands *today*.

I come now to the second particular. To *urge* you to make haste. Consider, what haste most people make in the world to sin against God, to break the commandments of their God. You have done this too. This has been your practice. O! what haste you have made to sin! How fast do many men swear! How often are many men drunk! How with great haste many run to their wicked friends. How fast does the adulterer and fornicator run to his harlot! Shall others make haste to hell, and will you not make haste to heaven! Shall others make such haste to provoke God, and will you not make haste to please your God? Here we cannot make you to be slow. Here we would gladly have you to stop, to stay and to please God, but you will not do it. If we gather arguments from God, from the wrath of God, from the justice of God, to stop your course in sin, yet, you will still go on. If we gather arguments from the promises of God, from the threatenings of God, both in light of all this, the sinner will make haste to continue in his sin. It does not matter if we tell you that sin is the way to hell, and the undoing of your souls. For all this, you will

A Call to Delaying Sinners

run into hell. Are you afraid that you cannot get to hell soon enough, or sure enough? Behold, you that make haste to sin, I call and cry this day, "Why such haste, sinner; why poor sinner, why such haste? Why do you hasten so fast to run on in that course that will certainly bring you to that place of torment? Stop your course, stay sinner, turn back, the place that you are hastening to, is not a pleasant place; the torments that you are hastening to, are insufferable torments; turn back again then to God, and instead of making haste to sin, make haste to God." Believe me, sinner, believe me, if that you go to hell forty years from now, you will find that you are there soon enough. Why then should you make such haste? Oh, it is the blindness of men's hearts that make more haste to damn their souls, than to save them; that make more haste to hell, than to heaven; that make more haste to devils, than to God! That sinners make haste to sin, you have proof enough in your life, in your own observation, besides the Scripture. Proverbs 1:16, "Their feet run to evil, they, make haste to shed blood." Proverbs 7:23, "The sinner maketh haste as a bird that hasteneth to the snare." Mark 6:25, Herodias' daughter made haste to bring a charge to have John the Baptists' head on a platter.

  To press you to make haste consider, what haste most people in the world make to be rich on the earth; as if God sent men on the earth to mind nothing so much as the riches of this world. Do you not see men make haste to get the world, as if they could not be happy without it? As if they were undone if they were not rich! Why do these people make haste for riches, and will not you make haste

Sermon 4: Stop Your Sinning

to find Christ's grace? Tell me, is not grace better than riches, and God, better than gold? And are not the joys and happiness of the unseen world, a great deal better than the outward enjoyments of this present world? Take Solomon's counsel, Proverbs 3:14-15, "Wisdom (meaning Christ) is better than rubies," and all that the heart can wish or desire, are not to be compared to him. In Phil. 3:7, there Paul counted all things "but dross," and no better than "dung," in comparison of Jesus Christ. Ah sinner, when death shall come, and you lie on a bed of sickness, if your conscience is then awakened, or if not, then at the furthest, when you shall lie in flames, you will cry out for your folly, and say, "Oh wretched sinner that I was, that made such haste to get the world, but no more haste to get the favor of my God, that made such haste to get silver and gold, but, made no more haste to get the favor of God, and an interest in Christ."

Yet consider, when man fell into misery, and was a lost creature, the blessed God *made haste* to help him out. When man had rebelled, mercy made haste to pardon. When man had lost his way to heaven, the God of heaven made haste, and came himself, and preached the way of salvation to him. Oh how wonderful! That God should make haste to man, and yet, man will not make haste to God? That God should make haste to come and help man, and yet man will not make haste to accept this help! What would have become of mankind, if God had delayed, if mercy had delayed! But mercy *was on the wing*, mercy fled away quickly towards fallen man. The very same day that man sinned, God made haste, that very day, to come and preach a Savior to him. Read Genesis 3:7-8 with verse 15. There you read of Adam's sin, how he had sinned, and it is said, "In the cool of the day, God came making haste, to find out lost Adam, saying, "Adam, where art thou?" The God of heaven came to look after the sinner! As if he should say, "Is this the man that I made in my own image, and he has become liable to my wrath, subject to my curse, and to the torments of hell forever! O! my heart yearns, I must make haste to convince him of his sin, and then to preach a Savior to him." In Genesis 43, Joseph made haste, for his heart yearned towards his brethren, and he looked for a place to weep, and he entered into his chamber and wept there. So, God does this with a heart towards lost poor sinners.

    To press you to make haste, the time is coming, when you will be in that case, that you will cry and call to God to come and help you. What do you think, sinner, will sickness never come to you? Will you never be in great pain? Shall your time of dying never come? Yes, it will, *it will*, and it is a hastening death. When you are full of pain with some disease, if you cannot rest on your bed, Oh what will your sayings then be? "Oh that God would make haste and ease me, and give me some relief! Oh this sickness I cannot endure!" This will be your request not long from now. And when you hear God's response, it will break your heart. It is as if God should say to you in your distress, as now you say to God in your prosperity, God says, "make haste to come to me." "Yes," you say in your heart, "next year I will, or after ten years, then I will." Then, what if you, when under such pain, would cry to God, and say "Help

Lord!" Then God should say, "After one year, or ten years, then I will, but until then, you will lie there in your distress." Psa. 40:13, "Be pleased O Lord, to deliver me, O Lord make haste to help mem" and verse 17, "You are my Help and my Deliverer, make no tarrying O my God." You do not want God to delay one day longer, not one hour longer. You would begin and end your prayer in your distress, with this request, "Make haste Oh God to help me," as the Psalmist does in Psalm 71:12, "O God be not far from me, O God make haste for my help." Even evil Pharaoh will cry for help, when judgments are on him.

All the provisions and preparations that the blessed glorious God has made to welcome sinners, when they come to him, all cry aloud to you, for you to make an earnest haste towards God. The eternal God has made a great preparation for you. This blessed God invites you. Sinner, make haste and come to me, for you will be damned if you do not. Oh sinner, make haste, and come quickly to me; you will perish forever if you do not come quickly to me. I have a pardon for you. Come to me, I have a heaven for you. Come to me, I have prepared a Kingdom and a crown for you, and behold, you will dwell with me forever. Though you have rebelled, I will pardon you if you will come to me. Though you have deserved hell, I will give you heaven, if you will come to me. Behold, this blessed God made haste to send his Son, and Jesus Christ made haste to come and die, the Spirit makes haste to come and move on your consciences and the ministers of Christ make haste to come and offer Christ to you. Now, shall God make haste, and Jesus Christ make haste, and the Spirit make haste,

A Call to Delaying Sinners

and ministers make haste, and will you not, then, make haste?

My next argument shall be, to consider your time that you have to come to God.

1. First of all, the time that you have allotted to you to come to God is short, and a little time. What is it but a few more years or months, weeks or days, and your life will be ended? Oh friends, consider where you stand! You stand on the brink of eternity, on the borders of another world. You are exceedingly near heaven or hell, and yet will you make no more haste?

2. This little time that you have, it is hastening away quickly. How swift does the sun and firmament move in the sky! Do you not see how one day and one night flies away after another, and one week, one Sabbath goes away after another, and your time is a hastening, whether you are drinking, or playing sports? Sinner, unless you can stop the sun's movement in the sky, do not remain in your sins any longer.

3. This hastening time, it is very uncertain as well, when it shall end. When an end shall be given to it. Sinner, can you tell that you will live until tomorrow? Let any man come forth that can say, "I am sure I shall live until tomorrow." Where is the one among you all that can say, "I am sure I will live for the next hour. I am sure that such and such a person will live for the next hour. I am sure that I will live this Lord's Day until the next Lord's Day." Can you say that of yourself or of another? Who knows, but you are keeping your last Sabbath, and hearing your last sermon? Who knows, but you are making the last

appearance in a public congregation right now? Do not boast in yourself of tomorrow, for you do not know what the day may bring forth. You will be found to be the tool of all fools, who does not know the way to depart out of this world, and yet you still delay in coming to the Christ. And you will not make haste to come to God.

4. Your time that is past, will never come again; if you would give a million dollars to regain yesterday to fix something, it cannot be recalled. Or for last Lord's Day, it cannot be recalled again. Consider your time, then, judge if it is not high time for you to make haste, and to delay no longer.

I want you to consider that all the time which you delay, you are abusing the mercy of God, and abusing the patience of God. Is this a thing to delay in? Does the eternal God stand still, and does not damn you, and call you down to hell at this very moment, which he may do at any hour at his pleasure? And does he tarry and not punish you? And do you tarry and will not come and submit to him? This God is entreating you to receive his mercy, and hates that you should perish, or lose your poor soul. Now he is offering the rich blessings, purchased so dearly, by the blood of his own Son Jesus Christ; and all the while you still neglect him. What do you say in your heart, "I don't really care for God, or for his Christ either?" Sinner, remember the time is coming, the hour is hastening, that you would give ten thousand worlds if you had them, for that grace which you now despise. The book of Romans talks about you despising the goodness of God in the word, not considering that the patience and longsuffering of God should lead you to repentance!

Your delaying has in it a great deal of bold, and blind presumption. You presume of such things that you have no grounds to make good on. There are three or four things that a delaying soul presumes about.

1. You presume that you will live even in light of the danger. You presume, that you have more time to spend in this world. You suppose that you may have another year yet, another month yet, another week still. Tell me, isn't this what is really in your heart? "I have time enough to spare!" You are worse than a mad man indeed, that will not make haste and come to Christ. You believe a very bold presumption. You talk about life a year from now, when you do not know if you have even another hour. Who shall die on the spot? Who shall suffer a heart attack? Who shall have an aneurism, or be killed in some strange accident?

2. You presume, that you can repent whenever you want, and turn to God whenever you want. You presume that your own will is of your own strength. But know, either you can repent whenever you want, or you cannot. If you can, and don't do it, you are inexcusable. But if you cannot repent right now, do you think you can repent better afterwards, when you have hardened your heart even more in sin?

3. In your delaying, you presume that the Spirit of God will help you afterwards, as well as now, because if this were not your hope, if you did not think about that, if you have not left off your understanding, you would repent right now, while the Spirit of God is moving on your heart?

How do you know, but afterwards the Spirit of God may leave you alone, and give you up to the hardness of your own heart? God may say to you, as to Ephraim, Hosea 4:17, "Ephraim is joined to idols, let him alone." Ah, sinner, if God says once, "Let him alone," then all the sermons in the world will do you no good at all. If God would say to the delaying sinner, "My Spirit, let him alone, and my ordinances, let him alone, and my ministers, let him alone, what then?" That though you have the voice of the Gospel in your ears, yet God will let your heart alone. What a terror that is.

And the last argument to persuade you to make haste, is this, it may be you may be hostile to hear it. But, I wish, sinner, that by yielding to all the rest, you would give me a reason to forbear to speak about it. But if all that has been said will not move you to make haste, then know that your damnation is hastening, the time of your lying in torment is hastening, the hour of your being thrown down to devils, and lying in chains of darkness, is hastening. Sinner, though you are asleep in all this, yet your damnation does not slumber. 2 Peter 2:3, "Whose judgment now of a long time lingereth not," and there damnation does not linger. You linger, and you waste time, yes, but your damnation does not sleep. Consider, Deut. 32:35, "To me" God says, "belongeth vengeance and recompence; their foot shall slide in due time, for the day of their calamity is at hand, and the things that shall come upon [you] maketh haste." I end with this, make note of it, that your calamity is at hand, and the thing, the wrath of God that shall come on you, makes haste to run after you.

A Call to Delaying Sinners

The justice of God that shall overtake you, makes haste to run after you; and you will be caught if you do not repent and turn to Jesus Christ. O! then, if you would make haste to escape all those dreadful things that are hastening, make haste, and do not delay to keep the commandments of your God.

Sermon 5
Young and Old

Psalm 119:60, "I made haste, and delayed not to keep thy commandments."

I have given you many arguments and motives; and if I thought that you had made haste and come away to Christ, I would change my text and go on another subject. But are people so eager to hasten after God? Because of this, I want to put you on hastening directly, with a direct exhortation to five sorts of people. I will describe these five and then explain them each.

First of all, I would persuade such of you as are young, that you would make haste and not delay, even you that are children, little children, the youngest among you that understand what the sense is of any of these things. O! do you run quickly to Christ? Make haste young ones, in your youth; make haste and do not delay.

2. I would direct this exhortation to such of you as are old, old sinners, for God's sake, make haste, you that are sixty or seventy years old and more, make haste.

3. To such of you as are strong and healthy in your body, make haste.

4. To you that are sickly people, often sick and seldom well, for God's sake, make haste.

5. To such of you as have been sick, and now are well, as have been on beds of sickness very near to death,

but God has set you on your legs again. Make haste, and do not delay to keep the commandments of God.

First then, you that are young, you that are yet in your childhood, you young children, you young boys and girls, do you make haste, and do not delay to keep the commandments of God? I would rather press this counsel on you, because you, of all people, chiefly lie under the temptations of delay. For you children, have very naughty hearts, and hate to be good, to come to God. You are apt to think, that you still have time enough. You can take your pleasure and mind your sports and entertainment now, and think of God afterwards, and think of heaven and hell afterwards. But I have *ten questions* to propose to you, you young ones, and by the time that I finish these, I hope you will see that there is no reason for you to delay to come to Jesus, though you are young.

1. Tell me, are you so young that you may not die? Are you so young that you may not become sick? Are you young men exempted from death and the grave? Have you not seen, that as young as you are, and younger too, young children have gone down to the grave? Have you not seen or heard that little infants are also carried to the grave? Have you not seen infants laid in the dust? Have you not seen many times that there is but little difference between the birth and the grave? If you doubt this go into some churchyard, and see if you may not find there graves of all sizes; an infant was buried here, another young one was buried there, who was not so tall as I am you might think. You may be very young, but you are not so young to not

die, and are you so young then, that you may not make your peace with God?

2. Are you so young that you may not be damned? Has God anywhere told you in his word, that no young ones shall go to hell, those that die in their youth? Tell me, were you not born in sin? And are you not by nature children of wrath? And by reason of that sin in which you were born, are you not liable to the wrath of God, to the damnation of hell, and to the torments of the damned? Besides, don't you, young men, have many sins of your own committing; actual sins? How soon did you learn to lie? How soon did you learn to take God's holy Name in vain? How soon did you play on the Lord's Day, and so misspend your precious time? By all these you deserve death and hell too. And if you are not so young, but you may be damned, is there any room for you to delay to come to Jesus, and not to do what God commands you to do?

3. I pray, tell me, is it fit that you should give the first of your time to the devil, rather than to God? For you first to serve the devil, then next, to serve God, to give your youth to the devil that would devour and destroy your souls, rather than to God, who would save your souls, and make them happy? Should you give to the devil the first of your time, who deserves none at all? And, I tell you, that you deserve to be damned, if you give one hour to him. Think of it, what would the world think of you if you deal with your parents as you deal with the eternal God? If you should say, "Father I will rebel against you, though I am young. I will displease and grieve you, while I am young. But, I will be dutiful to you when I am old." Will you, in

effect, say something worse to God? And say, "we will do what the devil says to us now, and we will do what God commands for us afterwards." Tell me, who was it that gave you being? Who was it that formed you in your mother's womb? Who was it that brought you forth? Who was it that preserved you, while you hung on your mother's breast? Who is it that kept you from death and hell to this day, that might have cast you into utter darkness, as soon as you beheld the light of the sun? Has the devil done for you as God has done or can you expect he shall or will? Put all these things together, and think about it, is it better and more fitting that you should serve the devil first in your youth?

 4. Tell me, you who are young, can you be good too soon? Oh, can you have your God too soon? Oh, can you mind your souls too soon? Can you be mindful to the torments and the damnation of hell too soon? Can you be sure too soon of heaven? Tell me, would it do you any harm to know at a young age that your soul shall be saved? Would it do you any harm to believe in Christ, to love God above all, and to understand, whenever you will die, that your soul should be received into heaven? Remember this, that there have been many who have been troubled that repented as well, but there was never one in this world that ever repented too soon. Thousands, even millions, have wept and cried that they have rejected Christ for too long.

 5. Is not being young the usual time for God to convert sinners to his Son? This is true especially, those whom he plants under the Gospel in the time of their

youth. Oh, you that are set under preaching, if you are not converted while you are young, it is a thousand to one, if you will *ever* be converted. Friends, consider, is it usual for God to convert *old* sinners? I know, God sometimes may call a person at the eleventh hour, yet, it is but here and there one, now and then, and are those commonly, people who did not sit under the means of grace when they were young. If you delay while you are young, you may let slip the very season of conversion, then your souls cannot be brought over to God by all the preaching in the world. Do we not among ourselves observe, that for one old person, one old sinner, that is made sensible of sin, and of his lost state, though he might not even be very wicked outwardly, that desires the prayers of a congregation for them, do we not have two, or three or more, that are younger, that are sensible?

6. Will it not be easier for you to repent now, than it will be afterwards, when by a long continuance in sin, you have hardened your hearts, and seared your consciences and have been accustomed to act wickedly? Certainly, now, while conscience is tender, and the heart more tender, it will be easier for you to let go of your sin now, and to let go of your wickedness now, than it will be forty years later; for the longer you continue in sin, the stronger is sin on you, and the stronger your sin is, the harder your heart is, and harder will be your repentance. "Can the Ethiopian change his skin, or the leopard his spots? then may ye also do good, that are accustomed to do evil," (Jer. 13:23).

7. Shall you not prevent a multitude of sins, if you make haste in your younger years to come to God? Where, if you go on in your sins, what a multitude of sins, how many thousands of sins will you add more and more to the sins that you have already committed? If you still delay, how many prayers will you neglect? And how many Sabbaths will you profane? And how many lies will you tell, which will not bother your conscience? And how many promises may some of you swear? Where, now, if you would come to God in your youth, if you would now believe and repent, and come to God, O! what a number of sins may you prevent the commission of! And isn't this more desirable? You have sinned enough already, the youngest among you have sinned enough already, you do not still need to go on and add more and more to your sins. For you can hardly number them already.

8. Consider, will not this be most pleasing to God if you hasten in your younger years to come to him? The time is early. Christ indeed loves young ones, when they will be good. Mark 10:23-24 is about a young man that had some common good in him; and it is said, "That Christ looked upon him and loved him." Jer. 2:2 says, God to Israel, "I remember the kindness of your youth, the love of your espousal." You see, God takes it kindly, and Christ takes it kindly, when you believe on Christ, and leave off all your sins. Oh, will you not do that which God and Christ will take kindly at your hands! Then make haste while you are young, and do not remain in sin until you are old. It is pleasing to God to see young ones come and pray, and believe, to see young ones following after Christ. I

Sermon 5: Young and Old

remind you of Eccl. 12:1, "Remember your Creator in the days of your youth." Now tell me, young men, is it not better for you to be pleasing to this blessed God while you are young, than to be provoking him until you are old? Is it not more pleasing to have his love and his smiles, than to have his anger and frowns?

9. If you make haste while you are young, shall you not have more time to serve your God, and glorify your Maker? And is this not the end for which you were born? Is not this the end for which you were made, that you may glorify him that gave your being to you? And tell me. Can you begin this work too soon? Or, can you do this one thing too much? Oh, young men, think, will God save you when you die, and will you not serve him while you live? Will God glorify you hereafter in heaven, and will not you glorify God while you are here on the earth? Tell me, do you think you can honor God in a little time, and in old age too; as you may in a great deal, beginning from your youth, to your elder years? I tell you, that multitudes of good people on their death beds, when they have been going to heaven, they have been full of grief on this account, that they served God so lowly, and loved God so late; that are going to heaven to live with God, and did not do more for God when they were here on earth.

10. And lastly, if you now make haste while you are young, shall you not have more time to do the great work in your own souls that is to be done? O! what a great deal of work lies within us? What a great deal of work lies on our hearts to be done! On our souls! Is it not more likely that you should do more in forty-years-time, than in five or

ten, or the latter end of your days? O! how much knowledge is there to be had of God and of Christ, and the great mystery of the Gospel! You will have more time to get a greater measure of the love of God and of Jesus Christ; you will have more time to get assurance of the love of God and of eternal glory. You will have more time to make your preparation for death, and the great account that you have to give to God after death.

Now, take these ten things along with you, and then see, if there is any room or reason for you to delay though you are young, but make all the haste you can to do what God commands. That is the first sort of people.

2. The sort that I would urge this on, is also, you that are old. You old sinners, consider the work that you have to do.

1. Of all you that are old, do you make haste? For your time is almost gone, your time is almost run out, your sun is near setting; in a course of nature you do not have much time to live. Behold! look on your gray hairs, and they will tell you, that you are going off the stage of this world, and are entering into another world. The age of a man that most reach ordinarily, is seventy years or so. Psa. 90:10, "The age of man is threescore years and ten." You know people who have outlived this length of time. Some are seventy years and upwards? How near, how very near are you to another world who sit here! You are almost at your journeys end. What and sit still? You know some people that are so old you wonder at their age. When a person begins to be going onwards to eighty, people commonly wonder at their age. Can such people be delaying? Are you

Sermon 5: Young and Old

old to a wonder, and wicked to a wonder too? Consider, it is just a little while that you have to stay in this world; make haste, therefore, and do not delay.

2. You that are old, make haste; for some of you have not yet begun your work. What! And delay still, and be idle still! What do you mean? How many old ones are there, that have not spent one hour in sixty years heartily serving God? I am not saying you have not spent an hour in hearing and in praying; but some of you possibly have not spent one hour in *heartily* serving God. You are in a natural state and condition. What are you that are old, and never convinced of sin to this day, that are fifty, sixty, yes seventy years old, and yet strangers to the very first principles of religion! O! how sad is it to see gray hairs and ignorance! I have seen a child of five or six years old that has known more of God and of Christ than many that I have seen of fifty or sixty. And yet these old people sit still? Sirs, are you resolved indeed to go in this way to your grave? Are you resolved indeed to die and to be damned too? To see old people to be careless of God, and careless of their souls, negligent and slothful, what a shame it is? Age has forced you to lean on your cane, but it has not forced you to lean on your Savior. How we say of some, who are wondrously old, and yet wondrously wicked; wondrously old, and yet wondrous ignorant? Have every one of you that are old, fifty or sixty years old, have Christ in your hearts? Would to God you had; I wish you had. Have every one of you repented of sin? O! consider, what a thing this is, to live fifty years, yet be without God? To delay sixty years, and never come to God. To live until you come to that state in

which nature is almost consumed, yet have no faith? May not some of you say, that you have not shed one penitent tear for all your sins, no, not in fifty years' time; but you that are older, and have begun your work, yet there is reason why you should make haste to do more, and to go forward, and make greater progress still. You that have loved God and believed on Christ, tell me, do you think in your very conscience, that you have *so much* love to God, as you might have had in fifty years standing? Who can say yes to this? Is it that you have gained so much grace as you should have done in so much time, and as you should have done by the help of so many means as you have had in so many years? Make haste and do not delay! What do you think, you that are old, you that I may call my father in age, what do you think, are there not some that are twenty years younger than you, forty years younger than you, that love God, and fear God, and hate sin *more* than you do? Is this not a sign that you have delayed too much? O! therefore make haste and do not delay any longer.

    3. You that are old, make haste, and do not delay; for haven't you lost enough time already, but you must lose more still? Have you served the devil enough, and served your lusts long enough? Have not you forgotten God long enough, and neglected Christ enough? Heaven, and your souls, you have neglected long enough already, but still do it, and will you proceed to do it, and will you do it until you die? What do you mean you old swearers, and you old drunkards, and old Sabbath breakers of God and haters of God and godliness, do you mean to rebel to your dying day? Do it a little longer and you will. Do you mean to give the

devil all your time, and all your strength? You that have lived sixty years, I fear should if you were allowed to live another sixty, you would do so still; you that have lived fifty years, I fear, should you live fifty years longer, you would still be the same. Sinner, are you resolved to go to your grave without Christ, without a heart changed? If you do, shall you not also go to hell too, and to devils too? What you do, it must be done quickly, or else it will never be done. For you will die before it is done. Shame on you, sirs, shame on you, to love God after so long time, shame on you. Shame on you to love Jesus Christ after so long time. Do you not have fear that you cultivate a great deformity of sin in your soul after so much time that you have spent in sin.

  4. You that are old, make haste and do not delay; for if you die old, and Christless too, if you die old and graceless too, the patience of God that has waited on you in your old age will aggravate your sin and your condemnation too. I tell you all, that much of you had better to have died in your childhood, than to have lived to an old age; you had better have died as soon as you had been born, than to have lived so long, and go to hell at last; you had better have died when you could not go, by reason of infancy, than to live until you could not go, by reason of age, and die *out of Christ* at last. If you die old and wicked, old in your sin, hell will be hotter when you go there, though it is longer until you go there; will you yet delay? O! you that are old, I pray you make haste, and do not delay any longer.

  5. And lastly, I pray you make haste and delay no longer; for, tell me, can you give an account of your

misspent time already? You shall certainly be called to an account for every year you have had, for every month you have had, for every week, day and hour that you have had. Time is going and you must be called to an account how you have spent your time. Can you give an account to God of fifty years spent in ignorance, not knowing God? Can you give an account to God of sixty years spent in a natural state, in which you knew nothing of God nor did you ever do one hearty duty to God in all this time!

O! you that are young, you are my hopes! I profess that I have more hope of you, than of those that are old and wicked. I take it to be my great advantage, that I preach to so many that are young; think of what has been said to you, and what has been spoken to you, and when you come home, consider, you have heard ten things, that there is no room for delaying; and you that are old, if you are not past feeling, O! would to God you were not. This is the mischief, when people are young, then they think it is too soon; and when they are old, then they say, they have been of this opinion ever since they were born, and they will not change now. Well, think what you will, but you must change, or, you must be condemned. You would think it hard to wait on a fellow a day, or week when they say they were coming; yet this blessed God has waited on you so many years. Make haste and come to God, and do not delay any longer.

3. To you that are strong and healthy, do you make haste and not delay to do what God commands you, though you are strong and healthy, yet make haste and do not delay. You have need of this advice, because being

strong, and in perfect health, you are apt to put away the day of death from you, and repentance too, and Christ too; and making your peace with God, because you are not full of pain, and God does not often cast you on beds of sickness. So, you think there is *no need* for you to make haste.

First of all, as strong and as stout as you think you are, many have been cut off in a week's time, and less; so, make haste; as strong as you are, when death comes it will make you cry out, "Oh I am sick, I am sick; I am pained, I am pained!" It will make you to tremble. You see often times that sick people out-live those that are of a healthy constitution. Do not venture your soul's eternal state on it because you are strong.

2. Tell me, who is it that gives you your strength? Is it God, or Satan? If it is God that gave you your strength; what a disingenuous sinner you are to God, that because God does not fill your body with pain, so you will fill your body with sin? What does God give you health for, and give you strength for? Does God make you strong, that you may be strong to sin, and spend your days in sinning against him?

3. Consider, which is the fittest time for you to repent, and to make your peace with God, now, when you are well and strong, or when you shall be sick and near death? How often I have seen people on their sick-beds unfit to talk, that put off their repentance until at last, until they were sick. Then sickness brought its burden with it, its excessive pain with it, that they had no mind to speak

about any such things. That is the third sort; to those that are strong.

4. My exhortation also is to such of you as are sickly and of a weak body, that are often sick, and often ill. It is time for you to make haste, that live in daily expectation of another world, that daily look for your last day, and when your last hour will come, and when you shall draw your last breath. How often has God taken you, so to speak, and shaken you over your grave? How often have you been in that case on your sick bed, that men could not tell, whether you will live or die? And now God has restored you, yet you are still weak and still sick. Is it not time for you to make haste? Behold! The voice of every sickness is, "Sinner, make haste." The voice of every affliction is, "Sinner, make haste."

5. And lastly, my advice is to such as have been sick, and now are recovered; do you make haste and not delay to do what God has commanded you to do? Will you sin again as you did before? Will you slight Christ again, as you did before? And neglect heaven, and God, and Christ as before? Sinner, did God give you your life again, that you should rebel against your Maker again? Have you forgotten how your soul was filled with amazement and horror when you thought your life was so near to another world? How did you beg, and cry, and call, "O that God would restore my life this once! O that God would give me a little more time! O if God would recover me. I will become a new man, I will forsake my sinful companions, I will neglect prayer no more, I will profane God's holy day no more!" These were your promises; God has restored you again, and have you so soon forgot what you promised God, and do you delay

as much as before? Consider, and for God's sake, lay it to heart. Did you tell a lie to God when you were on your sick bed? Did you play the hypocrite with God, when you did not know whether you should live or die? Therefore, you that have been on the brink of the grave, and God bid you to look into eternity, and you saw you were not prepared, you begged him a little longer time, and God spared you, therefore, now, make haste.

I have exhorted such of you as are young, that you would make haste and not delay, even you that are children, little children, the youngest among you.

I have directed this exhortation to those of you who are old, old sinners; make haste, you that are sixty or seventy years old and more, make haste.

I have exhorted you that are strong and healthy in your body. Do not delay to come to Christ.

I have exhorted you that are sick people, often sick and seldom well, make haste.

And to such of you as have been sick, and now are well, as have been on beds of sickness very near to death, but God has healed you again, I say make haste, and do not delay to keep the commandments of God.

Sermon 6
Slow in Coming

Psalm 119:60, "I made haste, and delayed not to keep thy commandments."

    Now it may be thought, that I have said enough on this subject; but, I think I have never said enough on any subject, until I have gained your hearts to do what I have preached. Consider, how slothful many men are, how backward they are to come to God and how backward they are to believe, to repent and be holy. I think that there is enough reason to still consider what more is to be said, to press you to make haste, and I implore you to answer these following questions, and let your conscience answer as we go along.

    First of all, tell me, sinner, who is it that waits on you, while you delay? Is it not the blessed, and glorious, and eternal God? Is it not he that the angels of glory make all possible speed to do his commands? Is it not he, sinner, that might have damned you long ago, and cast you down into eternal torments, and you might this day have been among damned devils? Do you act in such a good way as to make God wait for you? Is it not he, that died for sinners, that is infinite in mercy to save you, if you come to him? Is it not he that is infinite in power to damn you, if you refuse? Is it not he, that is infinitely your superior Judge? Now, is there any reason for you to delay any longer, do it if you dare; do it, I say, at your own peril.

Secondly, who, or what are you, trifler, that this blessed God should wait in this way on you? If you consider you as you are a creature, or as you are a sinner, why should God wait on you one year after another? As you are a creature, is not your body made of dust, and must not your body not long from now, be turned into dust? What are you, but a better sort of clay? Do you not carry every day a dunghill about you, and must the blessed God wait on you? Besides, if we consider you, as you are a sinner, aren't you a hell-deserving sinner? Can't God cast you this day into hell if he wants, and into torments, even this very hour if he will? Can you be happy without his favor, and enter into heaven without his Son, and be saved without his mercy? Therefore, delay at your own peril.

Thirdly, what is it for, that this God waits on you? Consider, why does God give you so much time, one week after another, one month after another, year after year? Is it not to make yourselves rich in this world? Oh no, it is about a greater matter that God waits and stays? Is it not to see if you will mind your escaping eternal damnation! God gives you your time for this, that you may escape an eternity of torments: is it not for this that God waits? Think about it.

2. That God stays so long, is it not that you may mind the everlasting salvation of your soul in glory, that you may get a title to his Kingdom, that you may get an interest in his Son, that you may after all this dwell with him, with his Son, and with his Spirit, with his angels and saints, when you will be taken out of this world.

A Call to Delaying Sinners

3. Is it not that God waits, that you may be justified, sanctified, and pardoned? O! sinner, if God had not waited for this, he might have sentenced you down to eternal torments many years ago.

4. Is it not that God does wait, that of a captive to Satan, and to sin, you may be made free?

5. That you may be cured of your soul-sickness, and of those sinful diseases that are on your soul. Is it not for this, I say, for this that God waits on you?

Tell me, who shall have the worst of it, or who shall be the sufferer if you still delay, and do not make haste to repent, believe and be holy? Or who will be better if you make haste to be holy and repent? Who will profit from it, and who has the advantage? If you do not, the harm will be your own, and will not the wrong done also be your own? Sinner, do you think that God in this way waits on you, because he cannot be happy without you? Do not flatter yourself with this; for this God was happy before you were created, and if you are damned, this God will be infinitely happy and blessed without you. "Can a man be profitable unto God, as he that is wise may be profitable unto himself? Is it any pleasure to the Almighty, that thou art righteous? or is it gain to him, that thou makest thy ways perfect?" (Job 22:2-3). "If thou sinnest, what doest thou against him? or if thy transgressions be multiplied, what doest thou unto him? If thou be righteous, what givest thou him? or what receiveth he of thine hand? Thy wickedness may hurt a man as thou art; and thy righteousness may profit the son of man," (Job 35:6-8). It is a matter of admiration, that the blessed God should so wait long on sinners, or that the foolish sinner should so long delay to come to God.

Tell me, is it not life and death that is the issue of your delaying or making haste, yet will you loiter and delay, in respect of eternal life and eternal death too? If men will make haste in anything it will be where their lives are concerned; then they think it is time for them to make haste; there is no room for loitering then. When you are sick, how do you expect that all the people around you should act quickly? One makes haste and runs to the physician, another makes haste and runs to the surgeon, another makes haste and runs to the pharmacist. O! make haste sinner, your soul is in danger, your eternal soul is in danger? Do you not know, sinner, if you make haste and come to Christ, you shall have a life, a life of grace, and that is the sweetest life, the safest life, the surest life, the highest and noblest life, the most durable and lasting life. Such a life you can have, if you will haste and repent, and believe, and you will have a life of glory, to live with God, to live with Christ, to live with angels and saints. But, on the contrary, if you delay, death will be your portion, damnation will be your portion. And yet, do it all at your own peril.

Are you sure sinner, or do you know that God will wait on you one year, or one month, or one week more? How do you know but that this may be the very last hour or day that God will wait for your repentance? It may be God will say, "I will wait on you, sinner, no more, I will not wait one Sabbath more, I will not wait for one more sermon, for if you refuse now, I will listen to you no more."

A Call to Delaying Sinners

One wickedly said, 2 Kings 6:33, "Behold this evil is of the Lord, what, should I wait upon the Lord any longer?" To this, God may say, "this sinner still goes on in sin, still in the hardness of his heart, still in his refusing, why shall I wait *for him* any longer?"

Tell me, and let conscience judge you, and let your reason speak and give an answer, "Haven't you spent enough time in sin already, and yet will you not make haste to leave your sin? Tell me, sinner, is the devil's work so good, and his wages so desirable, and is the devil so kind as a master to you that you are so saddened to leave his service, and to come away from the service of your sin, to the service of God? Poor sinner! What did the devil ever do for you, or ever give you that you are so saddened to leave his service? If I ask you, how long since you were born? How old are you? One may say sixteen, another twenty, another thirty, it may be some say sixty. What? And are you graceless still! Out of Christ still! Is not thirty, forty, sixty years a great while to live in danger of hell? You young men, do you expect to be made free when you live in the service of the devil so long, and why don't you think it is not time right now to be made free? Oh think, "have I served sin twenty years, forty years, and is it not long enough?" Is this reasonable? It is long enough, and beyond all reason. Yes, sirs, how long will it be before you turn? God thinks that time is very long, and Christ thinks that time is very long, and the Spirit of God thinks that time is very long, and ministers think that time is very long, and all your godly friends, your godly relations would gladly have your souls converted, and saved. See how Christ thinks that it is a long time when he says, (Prov. 1:21-22), for Wisdom (that is) Christ cried out in the chief places, in the opening of the gates of the city. "How long ye simple and will ye love your simplicity, and fools hate knowledge?" *etc.* Psa. 4:2, "O ye sons of men, how long will ye turn my glory into shame?" Jer. 13:27, "Woe to you, O Jerusalem, will not thou be made clean, when will it once be?" So, God says to you, "Woe to you drunkard, swearer, unclean wretch; will you not be made clean, *when will it be?*

Have you not committed sins enough already? Have you not been drunk enough to answer already, but you will go on still, and still commit sins? Tell me, you that swear, have you not sworn oaths enough already? Have you not sworn so many in a day, so many in an hour, for so many years, and have not you sworn enough? Yet is it not time for you to leave off your swearing? You that have neglected prayer in your closet, and in your families? Have you not neglected things that should have been done? Have you not been guilty of omission? You that have been profaners of Sabbaths that go faster to hell on a Sabbath day than the whole week otherwise? Is not a hundred, a thousand Sabbaths enough for you to profane?

Seriously weigh, then tell me, is not the deserved punishment of your sin, that is due to you already, is it great enough, yet will you make no more haste? What do you think, will the pains of hell be easy pains, and the torments of hell be easy torments? Do you think, that the sins that you have committed, will not sink you deep enough into hell, and low enough? If not, then go on still.

A Call to Delaying Sinners

But alas, poor sinner, stop, for if the least sin should be inflicted on your soul, it will make you cry out and roar, it will make you cry, "I am undone, *undone*," it will make you gnash your teeth, and tear your flesh. Will one sin do this? What will then *all* these sins do to you which you have committed?

And lastly, tell me, have not multitudes and millions been damned already for delaying, and will you still delay? Will you not take all their damnation for a warning? How many millions are at this very time, sirs, while I am preaching to you and you hearing, in blackness and thickness of darkness, that if you could speak with them, you would hear them say, "Oh, it was our wretched delaying that undid us. We purposed to repent, but didn't. We purposed to go to Christ, to leave our sins, but woe to us, death came before that time, and we were damned before that time. Death came and drew us out of the world, and devils came and dragged us down to hell before that purposed time of repentance, and here we lie in the lake of burning brimstone, roaring and crying out and are undone." Now, sirs, have you so many millions been damned for their delaying, and will you still delay? Do it at your own peril.

Now, if I thought that there was never a delaying sinner among you, I would forbear, and go on some other subject. But, the Lord knows, I am afraid for you; and I have a godly jealousy over many of you, therefore I will try again, to conclude this text.

Has all that has been said from Sabbath to Sabbath, made you now to resolve to forsake your sins, and give up your heart and everything to God, and to Jesus Christ? O! that I had grounds to judge you! But I doubt there is one, and another, and another and many more, because their hearts are still yearning for sin. I will try yet once more.

I did propose ten questions to the delaying sinner overall, even to the children, and if you have slighted them, yet listen, sinner, again. I will propose ten more questions to you, and will you slight these too, and say that you will continue to do what you have done in the way you live?

First of all, tell me, poor trifling sinner, tell me, do you purpose in your heart, to obey God at all, or do you not? Do you intend to do the duty that God enjoins to you to do, or do you not? Say in your heart, "yes or no". You say to yourself, "I will wait here until you give your question," but I think it is a question that is so plain, that there is not a man that dares to have nerve to say, that he does not purpose to turn to God. Well then, here is my question, "Is it your purpose to repent of sin, and turn to God, or not?" If not, your purpose is nothing, the God of heaven pity you, and show mercy to you before it's too late. For, are you not a wretch indeed, that has not so much as a purpose in your heart to turn to God? If you said, "Yes, I do purpose to do what God commands," then tell me, "Why do you purpose that?" You are a rational creature, why do you purpose to obey God, and forsake your sin? Is it because you judge this to be your safest course? Is it because you think you must be damned if you do not do that? Is it because you think you cannot be saved? Is it because that God commands you? Are these your reasons? Behold, all the while that you delay, you are sinning against your conscience and your reason. For, your conscience tells you, it is your safest way to forsake your sin, and to look after Christ. Well, if that is so, (that it is best to leave your sin, and turn to God), why then do you not do this? If it is not best, why do you purpose to do it?

Secondly, are you purposed to do what God commands, to obey what he enjoins? What is it that you delay for, and do not do it then? Do you delay, sinner, to see if God will make new laws for you? Do you delay to see if God will give you an easier way to heaven, and salvation, than he has done already in his word? Do you wait to see if God will make laws which will be pleasing to you, that you must keep your sins and go to heaven too? Do not flatter yourself, he will never do it. If you wait forty years longer, the Laws of God will be the same then, as now, the commands of God will be the same then as now. If you waited forty years longer, you must repent at last, or you must be damned at last; you must believe at last, or you must go to hell at last. It is the same way that we are saved now, that Adam was saved then, and that Noah, Abraham, David, and Moses and the Apostles were saved, and all that are in heaven were saved by, that is, the way of holiness, and the way of faith in Christ, obedience to the commandments of God, being sanctified, loving God above everything. You must not think to dally with God, as with men in the market. In the morning you will barter and not buy, nor at noon, putting it off until evening, thinking then that the prices will all go down towards the close of the market. O! do not think that God will come to lower terms at the end of the world, or towards the end of your life. You may see, that God has prescribed the same things all along, Isaiah 53:7-8, "Let the wicked forsake his way..." Prov. 28:13, "He that covereth his sins shall not prosper; but he that forsaketh his sins shall find mercy." See, there must be a forsaking of sin, according to the old way of salvation. Ezekiel 18:31, "Cast away all your transgressions and turn from your sins," so inquiry shall not be your ruin. So in Christ's time, Matthew 3:8-9 and John 3:16. So in the Apostle's time, 1 Corinth 6:9-11. So it is still, and so it will be to the end of this world.

Thirdly, consider this too, and let your conscience reply whether you do well or not. Tell me, while you delay, do you not do worse with the blessed God, than you do with damned devils? I say, you deal worse with God. Do you delay in this way when the devil calls? Do you delay in this way when the devil tempts you? Haven't you the very same day, when temptation has been laid before you, yielded to it without delay, and listened to the voice of the tempter? When did you say to the devil what you have said to God a hundred times, when God has called you to repent, you have said in your heart, "not yet"? God has called you to believe, you have said, "not yet, Lord." God has called you, to believe on Christ. You have said, "not yet Lord." But when did the devil call you, and tempt you to sin, and you said "not yet?"

Fourthly, tell me, you that delay and do not repent, tell me, would you be served by your own servants, those that you have a power to command? And will you deal worse with God, than you would have others to deal with you? You fathers and mothers, if you command your

A Call to Delaying Sinners

children to do something for you quickly, would you take it well, if they should say, "I will not do it for twelve months," yet this is now ten years? If you that are bosses, command a worker to do something, and suppose the thing to be done is lawful, would you be content if he should say, "I will do it when I please, but not yet?" I know your hearts would rise, your passions would be raised up. Sinner, if God were not a patient God, would he have this at your hands? If God were not a patient God, would he have suffered his creatures to abuse him in this way? Consider with me here three things.

1. The distance between you and your children, you and your servants, is not so great, as between God, and you; not by a thousand degrees. No, it is not to be compared, as God is your Maker, infinitely above you, and you are not so much above a crawling worm, as God is to you. You cannot bear the delay of your children or workers and yet will you deal in this way with God?

2. Their dependence is not so much on you, as yours is on God. You workers have their food because they work and you pay them. But you have your being, your life, and everything from God.

3. Consider, that the work that God commands you to do is infinitely better than the work that you command your children or your workers to do. Suppose you set your workers about the work of their vocation, is this to be compared with everlasting work? If the work is menial for them to do, they do it quickly, because if they do not do it, you are angry. If you ask them to clean up their office, and they do not do it, you are angry. Behold, the blessed God

commands you to look after the cleansing of your soul, and the cleansing of your heart, getting an interest in Christ; and will you be angry if your workers will not do it for you, and will you delay doing what God commands?

Fifthly, tell me, delaying sinner, tell me, in all cases that concern you in this world, are you not dedicated to the present time? If you are sick, would not you be presently well? If in pain, would you not have something to presently ease the pain? When you are sick, if it is told to you, that you cannot have ease for twelve months, or three or four months, would this not be tedious for you to consider? Tell me, are you for riches and fame right now, and are those things your goals? Do you desire to be quickly rich? Would you not have a great deal of the world, you don't care how soon or fast? Or if you were in danger of death, or of your grave, how soon would you be helped, or delivered? And though you are in danger of hell, you make no haste to be delivered. You blind fool, you blind sinner, is not God and heaven, and Christ better than all the riches in the world? And is not hell more dreadful than the grave? And are you so eager after riches, and not after heaven? Do it at your own peril.

Sixthly, tell me, by these delays do you not put the greatest work that you have to do, on the greatest risk in the world? What have you to do in this world more than to make your peace with God, to prepare for death and judgment? What is there to do in this world more than to get off the guilt of sin, to get a holy heart? And yet to delay! You put everything at risk. I think your delaying to do what God commands is putting things to risk, is putting your salvation at risk, putting your damnation to be made sure by a loss of God, and of Christ. I think it is as if the sinner should say, "As yet, I will not obey the commandments of God, and I will risk it all for now. What issue will come up, really? I will risk it for now, and not seek after God, and Christ and heaven, and risk what may become of it." Alas, poor sinner! Have you anything else to risk?

Seventhly, will you in this way delay? Do not these delays prove to you that you love yourself and your sin better than the God of glory? You say, "No, I do not." No, why, then do you not forsake your sin, if you do not love it? Why then do you not let it go, when God commands? If you do not leave your drunkenness, and your uncleanness, and your wickedness, you shall not enter into heaven. Why then do you not let it go? If you love Christ indeed, why then do you not receive Christ into your heart? Will you pretend that you love Christ, when you will not have him come under the roof of your heart?

Eighthly, tell me, are not delays in these cases, arguments of great folly? And is it not a sign of the greatest wisdom for a man (in such cases as these are) to make the greatest haste? Is he not a madman, or a fool, that minds toys or trifles when he is in danger of losing his life? Are not you worse when you mind the toys and pleasures of this world, when you are in jeopardy of losing your souls?

There are five arguments to prove a wiseman. 1. That he is one that makes choice of the best good. 2. That he is one that takes care of the best part. 3. That he is one that walks in the best way. 4. That he is one that uses the best means. 5. That he is one that does all these.

This is the wise man, behold, God is the best good, your soul is the best part, the way of holiness is the best way, means appointed by God to get to heaven, are the only means. But on the contrary, to neglect these, it is a sign of the greatest folly. Will you do it still? Risk it all at your peril.

Ninthly, tell me, do not the delays of people greatly discourage the faithful ministers of the Gospel? Does not your delaying weaken our hands, and discourage our hearts, when we must study for you, and pray for you, and preach to you, and you cast it again in our faces? Do you think, that we can preach with life, when we see no fruit of our works? I profess, were it not for some of you, you would even tempt me to preach no more to you, were it not the command of God to continue my duty. You see, Isaiah 49:4, "Then I said, I have laboured in vain, and have spent my strength for nought and in vain," when he could not see the fruit of his preaching. So, ministers may say, "Lord, we have labored in vain, and have spent our strength for nothing, and in vain." Jer. 20:8-9, "For since I spake, I cried out, I cried violence and spoil, because the word of the Lord was made a reproach unto me: Then I said, I will not make mention of him, nor speak any more in his name." And by your delaying, when we come year after year, and preach month after month, and see many of you in your sins still, and walk in your wicked ways, do you think that this is not a great discouragement to ministers? And do you

A Call to Delaying Sinners

think, that God will not lay this sin to your charge, to weaken the hands of his servants? Do it at your own peril.

Tenthly, and lastly, do you not think, Oh delaying trifler, do you not know, that everything that you set your heart on, is hastening from you, and everything you love is hastening away, and yet, will not you make haste to get something that you may need, when all that now you love will leave you? Sinner, do you not know, that your time is going away, your health is going away, and that your life is going away; and yet will not you make haste? I tell you, know this, if you do not hasten to Christ sooner, without delay, you shall not before long be damned without delay.

Sermon 7
Isn't God Merciful?

Psalm 119:60, "I made haste, and delayed not to keep thy commandments."

You see, I have given you ten more questions in the last sermon. Has this done the work? Are you now resolved to go home, and enter into covenant to be the Lord's? Are you now resolved to forsake your sins and to let go of your iniquities? I doubt you are; some of you will still keep your sins, and will not come to God. Possibly, there are things still secretly in your heart, and they must be removed. Possibly you think, "Why Sir, why such haste? Is not God a merciful God, a long-suffering God? Is not God ready to forgive, and has he not promised so to do? And if I repent afterwards, won't God pardon me after? Why such haste then?"

I answer. 1. It is true, sinner, that God is a merciful God, otherwise, *woe and misery* would have been your case long ago. It is true, God is a patient God, a longsuffering God, otherwise you would not have been hearing a sermon now, but have been among devils and damned souls at this time. But what if it is that God is merciful, but you are now miserable?

Let me answer particularly. Tell me, first, are you sure that you will be alive at that time, when you purpose to repent? If the devil, or your own heart deludes you, now as you are young, to repent later when you are a man, are you so sure to live until you become a man? If not, where will your soul be then? Is it not then better to repent now without delay?

Secondly, are you sure to have the same means of grace then as now?

Thirdly, are you sure that the Spirit of God will strive on your heart, and move on your heart then, as he does now? If you are not sure, do not be deceived; for though God is patient, yet he may cut in two the thread of your life before you see those days where you intend to repent.

Fourthly, I suppose all that might be true, that you may live longer, and you may repent at last, and God pardons your sin at last. What then? Is this your ingenuity, to sin against God now, because you hope that God will be gracious and merciful to you afterwards? I thought you were a more ingenious person than that. Would you deal in this way with a friend, with a man?

But you say, what need is there for such haste? Some repent at the eleventh hour; all do not repent while they are young. To this I answer.

II. If some are brought in late in life, is it that most men stand out until then? No, it is but very few; it is a very rare thing to see people converted, and brought home to Christ at the eleventh hour. Sometimes God may do this, and truly it has happened, but it is only *sometimes*. How many do you know, that were converted when they were old, and sat under the means of grace while they were young? I suppose you can tell there has been very few. It is but *now and then*, and will you risk it, whether God will make you an example like that? I could never find it recorded in the Scripture, but of one man, that was converted at last, and that was the thief on the cross? I do not say that there were no others that may have been, but there are no others recorded in Scripture. Besides the thief on the cross, we only have this one other Scripture, "And about the eleventh hour he went out, and found others standing idle, and saith unto them, Why stand ye here all the day idle?" (Matt. 20:6). You object, that some came in at the eleventh hour. Consider, that Scripture, that is, those that came in at the eleventh hour, they were not *called* until the eleventh hour. Those that were called the third hour, came in the third hour. And those that were called the sixth hour, came in the sixth hour, and those that were called the ninth hour, came in the ninth hour. But those that came in at the eleventh hour, they were not called at the third, nor sixth, nor ninth, but at the eleventh hour. Now, what is this to you, that have been called a hundred times over, that have had call after call, and invitation after invitation? For when men are called at the third and sixth hours and do not come in, they seldom come in at the eleventh hour.

  What will you do, beloved hearers, shall I, after these sermons, and after almost a hundred things spoken to you, and all to this purpose to press you to make haste, and not delay, shall I go away from your presence and out of your sight, and will you turn your back on God, and say, "Yet a little longer, yet I must enjoy my pleasure, yet I must enjoy the world," as if you had no room in your hearts for God and Christ, or the things above? I would hope to prevail if I could with some on this one subject, whatever I should preach on, I should have the greater hopes to have you speed and hasten to keep those subjects too. Let me then give you a little more to move you.

First of all, if you would make haste and now keep God's commandments you would be blessed now, you would be happy now, and will this not make you to make haste? Tell me, have you a mind to go home happy, to go home with the love of God? O! If you would go home happy men and women make haste, do not delay any longer to keep the commandments of your God. Christ himself pronounces you "blessed," if you will but do this, Luke 11:27-28, "It came to pass as he spoke these things, a certain woman of the company lifted up her voice to him (that is, to Christ) blessed is the womb that bare you, and the pap that gave you suck." Ah, she says, what a blessed woman was that which bore this man! But Christ says, "Yea, rather blessed are they which hear the word of God and keep it;" that hear God's commands, and keep them.

Secondly, this keeping of God's commandments, would be an evidence to show your love to God. Would you like to know that you love God? Would you know this? Then do what God commands. Keep his commandments, obey his precepts, for by this you may know, that you love him, John 14:21, "He that heareth my commandments, and keepeth them, he it is that loveth me." "For this is the love of God, that we keep his commandments: and his commandments are not grievous," (1 John 5:3). Loving Christ's person, and keeping

Sermon 7: Isn't God Merciful?

of Christ's commandments, they usually go together. *Those that love me, keep my commandments.*

Thirdly, if you will but make haste to keep God's commandments, and believe when he commands, and close with Christ when he commands, God will make haste, and hear your prayer. When you pour out your prayer to God, "Oh Lord make haste, and do not tarry;" then God will make haste, and he will hear your prayer. Whatever we ask, we receive of him, because we keep his commandments by doing those things that are pleasing in his sight. Prov. 1:24, 28, "Because I have called, and ye have refused." Remember, that if you are dying, and should call to God for mercy on your death bed, if you should lie dying, when your soul is departing, and should call to God to save it, yet he would not hear your prayer if you neglect to keep the commandments of God. And for God to neglect to hear the prayers of a dying man, what a dreadful case is that?

Fourthly, if you make haste to keep the commandments of God, he will make haste actually to keep you when you are in trouble and temptation. If you would make haste to keep the commandments of God, God would make haste, and would not still wait beyond that hour that deliverance should be made for your good.

Fifthly, if you would make haste to keep God's commandments, it would be the readiest way that you could do, to have a blessing on your outward enjoyments. Just consider what God says in reading Leviticus 26.

Lastly, if you will do this, you shall be saved when you die. What do you desire more? John 8:51, "Verily, Verily, I say unto you, if any man keep my sayings, he shall never see death." That is, he shall never see eternal death, he shall never be damned. But you may say, "Sir, you press us to make haste to keep God's commandments; so you may, so we have; by your preaching you make us a disobedient congregation." I wish to God you were not. I say to you, have you kept the commandments of God? What does the passion we see in you mean? What does the pride we see in you mean? What does it mean, all the neglecting of prayer in your families, that we know of? What does the hardness of your heart mean, your slighting of Christ? What are the commandments of God? Is it not that you should repent? Acts 17:20, "now God commands all men everywhere to repent." Have you kept God's commandments? What! And not shed one tear for a thousand sins that you have committed? Yet do you say, that you have kept the commandments of God? The commands of God are that you should believe on Christ; turn and see, "And whatsoever we ask, we receive of him, because we keep his commandments, and do those things that are pleasing in his sight. And this is his commandment, that we should believe on the name of his Son Jesus Christ, and love one another, as he gave us commandment," (1 John 3:22-23). Now is Christ kept outside the door, and have you kept God's commandments? Is Christ kept out of your heart? Yet, have you kept the commandments of God? O! that you would do as you say! Make haste and do not delay any longer to keep the commandments of God.

Sermon 7: Isn't God Merciful?

In hopes that you will, I shall lay before you ten things, that will be the joy of angels, the rejoicing of ministers, and will make the heart of Christ content.

First of all, it is a blessed and joyful sight to angels, and to men, to see an offering God, and a receiving sinner; to see a tendering God, and a receiving sinner. In the Covenant of Grace, you may see God making offers to poor souls, making tenders to poor sinners; yes, making great offers and tenders of needful things to the souls of men. In the Covenant, God offers you grace, God offers you peace, God offers you his Spirit, God offers you his Son, God offers you his Kingdom, God offers you himself. What shall I say? God offers you all that you need, and God offers you all that you can desire. O! by this you may see on God's part, an offering and a tendering God. Yes, but let us see on the other side also, a receiving and accepting sinner. I think, sirs, that you should heartily receive what God offers you in the Covenant of Grace. I think you should say, "Oh Lord, do you offer grace to me? To me do you offer no less than yourself, and your Son and Spirit? Do you offer to me? Oh Lord I could never believe that you would offer any such offers to me, except I had found it in your word. Oh Lord, I will prostrate myself down at your feet, your Spirit I will gladly receive, and your Kingdom to be my portion." But, some will and some will not, (Job 1:11-12). Jesus Christ came to his own (offering himself to them) but his own did not receive him, but to as many as did receive him, to them he gave the power to be called the sons of God, to as many as believed on his name.

Secondly, it would be a blessed sight to see an inviting and admonishing God, and a coming and a praying, and a weeping sinner. In this way it might be, whenever this Covenant is entered into between God and man; God calls and invites, saying, "Sinner, here is mercy for you, you are on your way to death and destruction. That is not the way to eternal happiness that you are going in. Turn around sinner, and I will be your God, and I will show mercy to you." God does not only invite, but he pleads and expostulates the case with a poor sinner. "Why will not you accept of mercy? Why will you be so foolish to keep your sins? Turn, Oh turn, why will you die, Oh sinful soul!" This you find in Isa. 55:1, "Oh, every one that thirsteth, come ye to the waters; and he that hath no money, come, yea buy and eat; yea come, buy wine and milk, without money, and without price." This is God's invitation, and his invitations are *large*.

Every one of you that has a true desire, come; every one of you that has a longing soul after mercy, come. And it is made to those that have no worth nor worthiness in themselves, though you have no money nor worth. Yet, come, and you shall have everything made free to you. You shall have Christ free, and you shall have pardon free, and you shall have heaven free, without price. It is true, Christ did not obtain these things for men without price, his blood was the price to purchase these things; but there is no price for us to pay. We are called to come, and have everything free. What shall we have? There is wine and milk; milk for the needful, and everything necessary for you. But in the second verse, you have a pleading God,

"Wherefore do you spend money for that which is not bread, and why do you labor for that which satisfieth not? Hearken diligently unto me, incline your ear and come unto me." Hear this, God is on his invitation again, "Hear, and your souls shall live?" What is all this for? Now, in the 3rd verse, "And I will make an everlasting covenant with you, even the sure mercies of David." That is, "I will be your God, and you shall be my people," and all the pleadings of God with sinners, is for this.

In this way in the Covenant, you see an inviting, pleading God. O! that now, in the congregation, we could see a coming and a praying sinner? Oh, therefore say, whoever you are that has stood against the terms of mercy all your days and would have nothing of this God for your God, that never came into your mind ever since you were born, say, "Now Lord I come. Now Lord, since you are pleased to call and plead with me, behold, I come accordingly as you call me."

It would be a lovely sight to see sinners returning to an inviting God. Jer. 3:22, "Return ye backsliding children, and I will heal your backslidings: behold we come unto you, for you are the Lord our God." This is the coming of returning sinners; as God has pleaded with you, so you must now go and plead with God. O! it is a blessed sight to see a poor sinner pleading with God, that has been pleading with him; to see a sinner on his knees with sorrow in his soul, and tears in his eyes, "Lord, I am a poor miserable wretch, a hell-deserving wretch, and that many years since might have been cast into eternal torments, and this day I might have been among deplorable reprobates;

A Call to Delaying Sinners

but yet you have given me time to seek your favor and mercy. Now Lord, forgive my sins and renew my heart, and sanctify me throughout. Now Lord, I call to you, that you would enable me to turn, and enable me to believe."

Thirdly, it would be a sight causing angels and men to rejoice, to see a waiting God, and a hastening sinner. Indeed we see every day a patient God, and a long suffering God, we cannot look on a gray headed sinner, but we do see a patient God in the greyness of his hairs; we cannot see a person grown up, but this we do see, a patient and a waiting God. But it is but now and then, that we see a hastening sinner. I do not mean a sinner hastening to hell, and hastening to destruction, and hastening on the way of sin. No, these sights are too common; but a sinner hastening towards God, and towards Jesus Christ is what I mean. Luke 19:4-5, Jesus Christ passed by, and looked up to Zachaeus on the tree, and bade him to come down; and it is said, "That he made haste and came down, and followed Christ." God has not only given you a call, sinner, but he has stood waiting, but how long have you delayed? You have made many fair promises, "I will repent," and, "I will believe," and "I take God for my God," but you really do not do it yet. We do not see any among you to be hastening towards God, while God is patient towards you. O! that would be a joyful sight indeed to see you come! Say now, "Lord, Lord, you shall not wait an hour longer on me."

Fourthly, it would be a joyful sight to angels and men, to see a promising God, and a believing sinner. If this were done, the Covenant would be made between God and your soul; if God promises, and you believe the promises, then God would be your God. And then you would be one of his people in the Covenant of Grace. You do see God to be a promising God. "I will," God said, "be merciful to all your unrighteousness, and I will remember your iniquity and sins no more; I will put my Laws in your hearts, and cause you to walk in my ways." And there are multitudes of such promises like that. It was in this way with Abraham, when God came to make the Covenant with Abraham, Gen. 17:1-2, *etc.* "And when Abram was ninety years old and nine, the Lord appeared to Abram, and said unto him, I am the Almighty God, walk before me, and be you perfect. And I will make my Covenant between me and you, and will multiply you exceedingly. And Abram fell on his face, and God talked with him, saying, As for me, behold my Covenant is with you, and you shall be a father of many nations: Neither shall your name any more be called Abram, but your Name shall be called Abraham, for a father of many Nations have I made thee; and I will make you exceeding fruitful, and I will make nations of you, and Kings shall come out of thee. And I will establish my Covenant between thee and me, and your seed after you, in their generation, for an everlasting Covenant; to be a God unto you, and unto your seed after thee. And God said unto Abraham, you shall keep my Covenant therefore, you and your seed after you, in their Generation," etc.

  You read there of God's coming to Abraham; and says he, I make my Covenant with you; and in your seed shall all the nations of the earth be blessed. This was a promise made to Abraham when he was ninety-nine years old; as there was a promising God, so there was a believing

Abraham, Rom. 4:18-20, "Who against hope, believed in hope that he might become the father of many nations; according to that which was spoken, So shall your Seed be. And being not weak in faith, he considered not his own body now dead, when he was about an hundred years old; nor yet the deadness of Sarah's womb. He staggered not as the promise of God through unbelief, but was strong in faith, giving glory to God." A soul is enabled by God to make application of the promises to himself, and being certain then that he is a believing sinner, he answers to a promising God.

Fifthly, in order for you to become a covenant people, and God your Covenant God, it would be a joyful sight to men and angels, to see a commanding God, and an obeying sinner. In the Covenant there are commands as well as promises, therefore they must be performed as a duty, as well as participated in as a privilege. Deut. 4:13, "He declared unto you his Covenant that he commanded you to perform." This God comes forth with a commanding voice, as well as with a pleading, tendering voice. Now, as there is a commanding God, so if there were among you an obeying sinner, then the Covenant would be fulfilled. "By faith Abraham, when he was called to go out into a place which he should after receive for an inheritance, obeyed; and he went out, not knowing whither he went," (Heb. 11:8). God called him his friend, and from out of his family, and he did not know where he was to go. Yet, he obeyed God. But God has told you where you should go, yet you will not follow him! God has told you, that heaven shall be the place, an everlasting Kingdom; you shall have mansions above in bliss, and glory shall be the place that God will lead you to, yet you will not obey God.

Sixthly, to see a threatening God, and a trembling sinner; is a very delightful sight. Not in itself indeed desirable, but in order to close with God on Covenant terms; for as God invites a sinner to take him for his God, and waits on him, and promises him heaven, he will give it to those who will receive it? And as God commands him, and tells him to take him for his God, so God threatens man as well, very severely, if he will not come to Covenant with him. How frequently are these in the Gospel! "He that believeth not is condemned." "Except ye repent ye shall likewise perish." "Without holiness no man shall see the Lord." These things are to man's eternal sorrow.

You may see a threatening in this to those that will not perform this Covenant, Leviticus 26:11-12, "And I will set my tabernacle among you, and my soul shall not abhor you, and I will walk among you, and will be your God, and ye shall be my people." Well, but what if men will not, is there any danger to a sinner, if he will not take God for his God? Yes, there is, verses 14-18 of that chapter. "But if ye will not hearken unto me, and will not do all these commandments; And if ye shall despise my statutes, or if your soul abhor my judgments, so that ye will not do all my commandments, but that ye break my covenant: I also will do this unto you; I will even appoint over you terror, consumption, and the burning ague, that shall consume the eyes, and cause sorrow of heart: and ye shall sow your seed in vain, for your enemies shall eat it. And I will set my face against you, and ye shall be slain before your enemies:

A Call to Delaying Sinners

they that hate you shall reign over you; and ye shall flee when none pursueth you. And if ye will not yet for all this hearken unto me, then I will punish you seven times more for your sins," (Lev. 26:14-18). So God goes on in many verses; but is there any likelihood that a sinner will take God for his God until he trembles before this threatening God? Your conscience is seared, you make nothing to come up to Covenant terms; but where God threatens, and the soul trembles, then it is a sign that such a man will be brought into Covenant with God.

Seventhly, it is a blessed sight, causing angels and men to rejoice, to see a bleeding Christ, and a weeping sinner. In the Covenant of Grace, you may see the one bleeding Christ; for Christ bled to confirm the Covenant between God and man. He is the Mediator of the Covenant, and the Surety of the Covenant, and the blood of Christ, it is the blood of the everlasting covenant. So that on the one side, you may see, a bleeding Christ; but where is the weeping sinner? Where is the broken-hearted sinner? Where is the contrite, and the bleeding sinner? Could we but see this, the work done, God would be your God then, and you then one of his people. Zech. 12:10, "And I will pour on the House of David, and on the inhabitants of Jerusalem, the Spirit of grace and of supplication, and they shall look on me, whom they have pierced, and they shall mourn for him, as one mourneth for his only son, and shall be in bitterness for him as one that is in bitterness for his first born." Look, all you souls, and see how your sins have pierced the Lord Jesus Christ, until his very heart-blood poured forth. "O! that he should become a curse for

Sermon 7: Isn't God Merciful?

me! That he should die, that I might live!" O! was there ever such love, and was there ever such Grace! O! could we but see this, a weeping sinner answerable to a bleeding Christ, and, the match would be made. God would, be your God, and you one of his people.

Eighthly, it would be a blessed sight to see a striving Spirit, and a yielding sinner; and this it must be, if God ever becomes your God, and you his people. There must be both of these, a striving Spirit moving on your heart that must solicit you for your love and *woo* you for your consent, to take God for your God. This is what the Spirit of God oftentimes does. You have felt him working on your heart, moving on your soul at a sermon, saying, "Sinner, open up; Oh sinner, your danger is great, if you go on in your sins." The Spirit has been so powerful on your heart, that it has brought you almost to resolve. But if you would have this God for your God, you must yield when the Spirit strives.

Ninthly, it is a blessed sight to see a preaching minister, and a serious and a listening sinner. This is as the means appointed by God, to bring sinners into Covenant with God; therefore, ministers are ambassadors for God. We stand in Christ's stead, and in Christ's stead, to propose the terms of peace between God and man; therefore, to see listening sinners as those which have a mind to have God for their God is a blessed sight. "Send therefore to Joppa, and call hither Simon, whose surname is Peter; he is lodged in the house of one Simon a tanner by the sea side: who, when he cometh, shall speak unto thee. Immediately therefore I sent to thee; and thou hast well done that thou art come. Now therefore are we all here present before God, to hear all things that are commanded thee of God. Then Peter opened his mouth, and said, Of a truth I perceive that God is no respecter of persons," (Acts 10:32-34). See, people set themselves as in the sight of God under a sermon. And, what was it that Peter preached? Jesus Christ the Mediator of the Covenant.

Tenthly, and lastly, which is the fruit of all of this, it is a blessed sight to see heaven prepared and a sinner saved. This is the fruit of the Covenant, in your taking God for your God, and your becoming his people. This sight we shall see at the coming of our Lord, we shall see a heaven prepared. Yes, and we shall see sinners saved, see multitudes go into heaven. This we see as the fruit of this Covenant, "Then shall the King say unto them on his right hand, Come, ye blessed of my Father, inherit the kingdom prepared for you from the foundation of the world," (Matt. 25:34).

Now my advice to you all is, that you would take this God to be your God, and give up yourselves unfeignedly to be the people of this God; or woe be to the sinner, if there is a God, but he is not yours. If there is a blessed God, but you have no interest in him, it will be saddening for you instead of blessed.

Sermon 8
Take God for Your God

Psalm 119:60, "I made haste, and delayed not to keep thy commandments."

I have told you about Psalm 119:60, and to make haste. I have instructed you to come with haste to Christ, the Mediator of the Covenant. It is now or never. Repent today, stop your sinning, whether you are young or old, healthy or sick, strong or weak, stop your slowness in coming, make no excuses, now is the time to take God to be your God.

Now, for God's sake sinner, for God's sake, and for your own soul's sake, let me implore you, and intreat you, as ever you will find mercy at the hand of God another day, come and take this God for your God. Come sinner, come as yet, it is not too late; as yet mercy may be had; and as yet, grace may be found; while the day of mercy lasts, and while the day of your life lasts, come this instant, and do not run backwards, and say for all this, "I will still keep my sins."

Consider this, if you will not have God for your God, you will be condemned by the Covenant of Works, and you will be condemned by the Covenant of Grace. Think of this, you are condemned by the Covenant of Works. Gal. 3:10, "For as many as are of the works of the Law, are under the curse; for it is written, cursed is every one that continueth not in all things which are written in the Book of the Law to do them." Here is your doom, cursed is every one, man, woman, and child, every one, bond and free, master and servant, husband and wife, that do not continue in all things written in the Book of the Law to do them. Have you done so? Have you continued in *all* things? No, not in *one* thing. Then you see that you are condemned by the Covenant of Works. What is your cure then? "O! the Covenant of Grace must help me," you say. Yes, but you are condemned there too, John 3:18, "He that believeth on him is not condemned;" but ... yes, but there is a *but* in this verse, "but he that believeth not, is condemned already." For what? What, because he has broken the Covenant of Works? No, the Law condemns him for that, for the breach of God's commands, and for the Covenant of Works. What then? Because he has not believed in the name of the only begotten Son of God. The Covenant of Works, that will condemn you for not performing, and the Covenant of Grace, that will condemn you for not believing.

Oh I think I will be very saddened to leave you until I see some or other strict Covenant with God and hear you say, "Oh I see I must take God for my God, or else, I am lost and undone, and that forever; I am accursed by the Covenant of Works, and by the Covenant of Grace, the one for not obeying, and the other for not believing." It is in vain for us to flatter you, you must have this God for your Covenant God, or else, you will come under the power of the second death. Temporary death is nothing, if eternal death did not follow. See what follows death, Rev. 6:8, "I looked and behold, a Pale Horse; and his Name that sat on him, was death, and hell followed with him." Ah there it is! There is the thing that makes death terrible! Indeed, sinner, death not long from now, will get on his pale horse, and will be riding swiftly towards you; yes, but hell follows after. Were it not for this, death would be nothing; but damnation follows after death; and it will be the case of every one that will not take God for their God.

Let us consider a little what is in this eternal death, before you take God to be your God. I hope I and the Spirit shall work on some of your hearts. Consider, therefore, there are two things in this eternal death, and both of them exceeding dreadful.

I. Exclusion from the blessed God. Ah sinner, as sure as you hear my voice, will you be shut out, and excluded from the blessed God, and blessed Christ, and blessed angels, and blessed saints, if you do not take God for your God. Matthew 25:41, "Depart from me ye cursed," from me, from the blessed Jesus. O! How miserable must that man or woman be that must be sent packing away from the blessed Jesus. This is the punishment of loss; but if it were the loss of only your pleasures, and the loss of only your friends, that would be nothing. Ah, but what things will you lose, if you die before *God and your soul* agree? It will be the loss of a loving God, the loss of a blessed Redeemer; this will be the loss, and you would have been better to lose ten thousand worlds than this one God. And if you are not in covenant with God, *then:*

1. You will lose your soul. The loss of a soul, "what shall it profit a man, if he gain the whole world, and lose his own soul?" It is not a small matter that you may lose, if God does not gain your consent; it is a soul.

2. Consider, it is your *own* soul, sinner, that will be lost, if you will not consent to take God for your God. I would not be guilty of the damnation of another man's soul for all the world. Tell me sinner, would you ruin another man's soul? Then, why will you ruin your own? Whose soul will you mind, if not your own? And whose soul will you take care of, if not your own?

3. If you do not take God for your God, you will lose your *only* soul. Ah poor sinner, you have but one soul that must be damned or saved, and will you not take care of your own soul? O! take care and see to it, it is your only soul. Sirs, God has given to all of us only one soul, lose that, and you lose everything; if that is damned all is damned. I think these thoughts should move you to remember your darling, to remember your only soul, that when you have but one, you may secure the happiness of that one. In the body God gives us many parts by pairs, two eyes, that if we lose one, we may see by the other; two ears, two hands, two feet, that if we lose one, we may have the benefit of the other; but God has given men but only one soul.

4. It will be the loss of your precious and immortal soul. If it were the loss of a mortal soul that should die, and cease to be, it could not be so much. But when it shall be the loss of an *immortal* soul, that cannot die, that cannot cease to be, this makes your punishment the more terrible, that will not come up to the terms of the covenant. That is the first.

II. In eternal death is the punishment of sense. All manner of pain and torments that a just and angry God can lay on you to all eternity. If you are willing to take this God

Sermon 8: Take God for Your God

on covenant terms, he will make you happy; but if you will not, know to your faces, this day, that the eternal God will plague you forever, will be your Avenger and Punisher forever. Consider the names by which that place is called, where all that die without God, must be cast into. I will name but four or five of them, and those briefly.

1. If you die without God being your God you must go to prison, as sure as you stand here; so this place is called, 1 Peter 3:19, and by this the prison you read of, is meant the place of hell, and the place of the damned.

2. Every one that dies before God becomes his covenant God, must be cast into a place of darkness, into a place of utter darkness, Matt. 8:12, "The children of the kingdom shall be cast into utter darkness."

3. Every soul that goes out of this world before God is his God, shall be cast into a lake of burning brimstone, Rev. 21:8.

4. Every soul that leaves this world before God is his God in covenant will be cast into a furnace of fire, Matt. 13:42, where you see hell is set forth by a furnace of fire.

5. Lastly, it is indeed a place of torment, Luke 16:28, the rich man says there, "Oh send to my brethren, and tell them what I endure, that they may not come to this place of torment. O have mercy on me, for I am tormented day and night." Now what is this, for which you must be cast into such torments? What for, for refusing of God?

Why are you so loathe, sinner, why, to take this God for your God? Why, will he do you any harm? Besides, I might have shown how, that four things will make your case exceeding woeful? Four hopes that I would prevail with you, though it were but with one or two people, to come over to God, and will say, "Oh, I come with all my heart, to take this God for my God."

First of all, if you will not, your pains will be universal pains, all over your body, and all over your soul, no part of your body free, no part of your soul free; afterwards in hell, eyes, and head, and heart, and all the pains of hell shall be universal; *every part of your person sinned, and every part shall suffer.*

Secondly, they shall be extreme too, sinner. If you will refuse this God to be your God, he will inflict on you the extremity of pain. Now, to have pain all over, and to be all over in extremity, what a sad case is this?

Thirdly, they must be continual, without intermission; not sometimes in pain, and sometimes at ease; no, no, this is not the case of the damned. No, there is no intermission, not for an hour, not for one moment in hell. If you have a pain on your body for an hour or two, or in the night, and in the morning you have ease, what a refreshment is that? But for a person to lie under the pain of gout and stone, and night and day cries out, "No ease, no mitigation, not an hours rest all night long." Consider, what it will be not to have an hours rest to all eternity, not the least intermission!

Fourthly, as it shall have no intermission, so it shall have no cessation. Imagine if it were that such torment and pain continues only for a thousand years, then to have an hour's rest between, then the next thousand years to that, and a thousand to the next set, that would be happy tidings for those in hell to have an hour's intermission each thousand years. But those that will not have God for their God, they must have pain without ease, and without intermission, and that forever.

But for one thing more. Besides all this, if you will not have this God for your God, your covenant God, you will have something to torment you in hell, that thousands of others never shall. Shall I tell you, beloved hearers, shall I tell you, you will have something to torment you, that devils shall not have. I say, something lies heavier on you than on devils; something to torment you, that the heathens do not have to torment them. What is that? O! it is the gnawings of a never dying worm, for the refusing of an offered Christ, of mercy, while mercy may be had. When you shall lie in hell, if God does not prevent you, what will be the gnawings of your conscience?

I think I can hear poor damned wretches that have sat under the Gospel, accusing themselves after this manner. "It was for the violation of the covenant of works that I am in this place; but I might have had help in the covenant of grace; God was offered to me, and Christ was offered to me, ministers pleaded with me day after day; but my conscience said, this you would not do, I said no, to my dying day. Had I accepted of mercy, while mercy might have been had, I would have not needed to come into this place of torment. But, woe is me, the devils above me, never slighted such mercy as I have done! Woe is me, the thousands of heathens that are above me, never slighted such mercy as I have done! A Savior was never offered to devils; a Savior was never preached to the heathens. But I like a miserable wretch now, like a damned wretch now, might have had mercy, but would not. I might have escaped this place, but would not. Woe is me, now I am lost forever! Woe is me now, I am damned forever! My praying time is over! I might have had God to have been my God once, but now he will never be offered to me anymore." So you see this, it will be worse with you than with devils and with heathens if you refuse to take God for your God, and you do not give up yourselves to be his people. That what the blessed and eternal God commands us to do, is to be done with all possible speed, with all haste, and without delay. AMEN.

Appendix: A Covenant Made with God

I have here, recorded for you, a Mr. B, we will call him. He made a solemn covenant with God, privately drawn up by himself, and I found this which is his own manuscript. Here is what he *wrote:*

Oh! Most dreadful God, for the passion of your Son, I beg you accept of your poor prodigal, now prostrating himself at your door. I have fallen from you by my iniquities, and am by nature the son of death, and a thousand times more the child of hell by my wicked practices; but of your infinite grace, you have promised mercy to me in Christ, if I will turn to you with all my heart. Therefore, on the call of the Gospel I am now come in; and throwing down my weapons, submit myself to your mercy. And because you require, as the conditions of my peace with you, that I should put away my idols, and be at defiance with all your enemies, whom I acknowledge, I have wickedly sided with against you. I do here from the bottom of my heart renounce them all, firmly covenanting with you, not to allow myself in any known sin; but conscientiously to use all means that I know you have prescribed for the death and utter destruction of all my corruptions. And where I have formerly inordinately and idolatrously let out all my affections on the world, I do here resign my heart to you that made it, humbly protesting before your glorious majesty, that this is the firm resolution of my heart, and that I do unfeignedly desire grace from you, that when you shall call me to it, I may practice this my resolution, through your assistance, to forsake all that is dear to me in this world, rather than to turn from you to the ways of sin. And that I may watch against all its temptations, whether of prosperity or adversity, lest they should withdraw my heart from you, imploring you also to help me against the temptations of Satan, to whose wicked suggestions I resolve by your grace never to yield myself a servant; and because my own righteousness is but as filthy rags, I renounce all confidence in them, and acknowledge that I am of myself a hopeless, helpless, undone creature, without righteousness or strength.

And forasmuch as you have of your bottomless mercy offered most graciously to me, wretched sinner, to be born again through Christ your God, if I should receive you, I call heaven and earth to record this day. That I do here solemnly avouch you for the Lord my God, and with all possible veneration, bowing the neck of my soul under the feet of your sacred majesty, I do here take you the Lord Jehovah, Father, Son, and Holy Spirit, for my portion and chief good, and do give up myself body and soul for your servant, promising and vowing to serve you in holiness and righteousness all the days of my life. And since you have appointed the Lord Jesus Christ the only means of coming to you, I do here on the bended knees of my soul receive him as the only new and living way, by which sinners may have access to you, and do here solemnly join myself in a marriage covenant to him.

Appendix: A Covenant Made with God

Oh blessed Jesus. I come to you hungry, and hard bested, poor and wretched, miserable, blind and naked, a most loathsome polluted wretch, a guilty polluted malefactor, unworthy forever to wash the feet of the servants of my Lord, much more to be married to the King of glory; but since such is your unparalleled love, I do here with all my power receive you, and take you for my Lord and husband, for all times and conditions, to love, honor and obey you before all others, and this to death. I embrace you in all your offices, I do renounce my own unworthiness, and do here own you to be the Lord my righteousness; I renounce my own wisdom, and do here take you for my only guide; I renounce my own will and take your will for my law.

And since you have told me, I must suffer if I will reign; I do here covenant to take my lot as it falls, with you, and by your grace assisting to run all risks, with you verily confiding that neither life nor death shall separate you and me.

And because you have been pleased to give me your holy laws, as rules of my life, and the ways in which I should walk to your kingdom, I willingly put my neck under your yoke, and set my shoulders to your burden, and subscribing to all your laws, as holy, just, and good, I solemnly take them as the rule of words; thoughts and actions, promising, that though my flesh contradict and rebel, yet, I will endeavor to order and govern my whole life according to your directions, and will not allow myself in the neglect of any thing that I know to be my duty.

Only because through the frailty of my flesh, I am subjected to many failings, I am bold humbly to protest that unallowed miscarriages, contrary to the settled bent and resolution of my heart shall not make void this covenant; for so you have said.

Now Almighty searcher of all hearts, you know that I make this covenant with you this day, without any known guile or reservation imploring you, that if you spy out any flaw or falsehood in this, that you would show it to me, and help me do it rightly.

And now, glory be to you, Oh God and Father, whom I shall be bold from this day forward to look on you as my God and Father, that you have set down such a way to recover undone sinners. Glory be to you Oh God the Son, who has loved me, and washed me from my sins with your own blood, and are now become my Savior and Redeemer. Glory be to you, Oh God the Holy Spirit, who by the finger of your almighty power has turned about my heart from sin to God. Oh dreadful Jehovah, the Lord omnipotent, Father, Son, and Holy Spirit, you have now become my covenant Friend; Amen, so be it. And the covenant which I have made on earth, let it be ratified in heaven.

FINIS

Other Helpful Books by Puritan Publications

Captives Bound in Chains Made Free by Christ
by Thomas Doolittle (1632–1707)
This is a potent and biblical treatment of being freed from sin and bondage through the blood of Christ. Doolittle is alike a drill that drills into the conscience of the reader. This is a wonderful book on Christ's redemption for both believer and unregenerate to come and drink from Christ.

The Nature, Necessity and Character of True Repentance
by Zachary Crofton (1626-1672)
When you finish reading this practical work by Zachary Crofton on biblical repentance, you might say to yourself, "I've never repented." That's the kind of impact he is going to have on you if you read this work even in a cursory manner. Don't miss this important puritan work!

Directions for Improvement in Grace and Practical Godliness in Times of Extraordinary Danger
by Richard Alleine (1611-1681)
How should Christian's react in times of extraordinary danger such as the plague? Or the sword? Or famine? Richard Alleine explains in this timely treatise.

The Affects of Sin on the Soul
by John Dod (1549-1645)
In actions of good intent, Christians can still bear great sin which causes them harm, and causes God to act in judgment.

Delivered From All Our Sins
by Nicholas Byfield (1579–1622)

A Call to Delaying Sinners

What should a sinner first do in inquiring how to be rid of all his sins? Byfield (almost exhaustively) catalogs the Biblical sins which must be fully repented of during conversion before God. This is far different than the church pastor today who simply wants you to say the sinner's prayer. Byfield stands in complete opposition to this, and shows, biblically, how repentance ought to be sought, and what should be repented of. What Christian or God-fearer would not want to be rid of all their sins through Christ?

Discovering the Wickedness of Our Heart
by Matthew Mead (1630-1699)

Do you know the depth of the wickedness of your heart? Few Puritan works dive headlong into such deep waters as this work by Matthew Mead. Mead was present at the plague in London, and uses the means of that horrifying time to press sinners to repent, and cause Christians to wake up out of their lethargy. This is a powerful exhortation for one of the best puritan preachers of the day.

The Spirit of Prayer
by Nathaniel Vincent (1639-1697)

What is prayer? What is Spirit-filled prayer? What does it mean to "pray in the Spirit?" Vincent treats this subject carefully and biblically, showing the Christian what it means to pray in accordance with God's will and with power. This is an awesome puritan treatise on the doctrine and theology of prayer.

www.ingramcontent.com/pod-product-compliance
Lightning Source LLC
Chambersburg PA
CBHW022113090426
42743CB00008B/835